# earth god risen

**An Inner History of the Horned and Horny Ones**

## alan richardson

© Alan Richardson, 2017

First published in Great Britain in 2017 by Skylight Press,
210 Brooklyn Road, Cheltenham, Glos GL51 8EA

Part of the text was published in 1991 as *Earth God Rising* by Llewellyn Publications, Minnesota, USA.

All rights reserved. Except for the quotation of short passages for the purposes of criticism and review, no part of this publication may be reproduced, stored in a retrieval system or transmitted, in any form or by any means, electronic, mechanical, photocopying, recording or otherwise, without the prior consent of the copyright holder and publisher.

Alan Richardson has asserted his right to be identified as the author of this work.

Cover artwork by Rebsie Fairholm
Designed and typeset by Rebsie Fairholm
Publisher: Daniel Staniforth

www.skylightpress.co.uk

Printed and bound in Great Britain by Lightning Source, Milton Keynes
Typeset in Agmena Pro and Mr Eaves.

British Library Cataloguing in Publication Data:
A catalogue record for this book is available from the British Library.

ISBN 978-1-910098-00-4

*Richardson traces the presence of the male aspect of deity in Westerners through ancient Egypt and medieval metaphysics into modern mysticism and his own experience. This he does with scholarly skill and a pleasant fluency. A delight to read and a worthwhile asset to possess. So much has been written of our Primal Goddess that it is refreshing to read of Her consort, the Primal God — which the author eventually finds in himself after looking nearly everywhere else. Adventurous and fascinating.*

— William G. Gray

to
Suzanne Ruthven who always saw through me
but didn't seem to mind what she saw.
And that star-dusted sybil Melusine Draco for
much subtle inspiration over many years.
plus
Rebsie, Daniel and Basil for being insane enough to do this.

# CONTENTS

|   | Introduction | 9 |
|---|---|---|
| 1 | The Journey into Egypt | 15 |
| 2 | And Then Camelot | 42 |
| 3 | The Caves and Forests | 85 |
| 4 | And the Places of Sacrifice | 123 |
| 5 | The Time of the Wakening | 152 |
| 6 | Endings and Beginnings | 163 |

I wrote the first edition of this book half a lifetime ago when I was a somewhat pompous young man, pitching it largely to the American market, and called it *Earth God Rising*.

I started it while living in a small rented gardener's cottage in the grounds of Murhill Manor in the sheltered depths of the Limpley Stoke valley, and finished it when we moved to a less small but windswept house on the top of Winsley Hill. It was written in the days before the internet, word processors, emails and all those things which make writing a comparative doddle today. All my research had to be done via awkward trips to the nearby town, hoping that the notional entity known as the Library Angel would approve of my atavistic concerns and point me to the raw, simple details I needed. It always did.

The energies of the Horned Gods undoubtedly raged inside me when I started that first version. At one point I was so 'lost' to what was flowing through that my wife, not unreasonably, had a right go at me in the checkout at the supermarket when I was too dream-wasted by impulses from ancient and near-forgotten deities to help with the very necessary (and far more important) task of packing the bags with our groceries.

Horned Gods being what they are, they pushed me toward a deliberately simplistic approach to magic. This was partly because I was driven by a statement of the old Gnostic Basilides: *It is only through Ignorance, in conjunction with Silence, that the royal road to liberation can be found.* I liked that statement then, and adore it now. For me it is up there with a comment made about the well-hung but taciturn movie star Gary Cooper: *He don't say much, but when he do… he don't say much.* Whether I fully understood what Basilides (who later manifested through Carl Jung) was really saying, or whether it was an excuse for not being smart enough to enter academia, I do not know. But the horned and horny ones took me in hand and showed me things – wonderful things – in their own silent and apparently ignorant ways.

Re-reading my book now I was startled by how much I seemed to know in those days, as the pages poured out information that struck me as completely new. I felt a bit like Little Jack Horner (a very real character from the nearby village of Mells) who once put in his thumb and pulled out a plum and exclaimed 'What a good boy am I!' Fortunately, I was stopped from being too smug by the fact that certain things I wrote then, while not being totally 'wrong', have been modified by the passing years. Whether this means that I have increased in wisdom, or that my balls have withered and shrunk, I leave it to the new generation to judge.

In some ways this fascinating, ageing process of mine is like raking a Zen garden. My own Zen garden is surrounded by a very low wall of red brick and is about 9' square. But because it only exists in my head, it is infinite. It is filled and levelled with a mass of pebbles, each one representing an experience. While most of these are grey gravel chips, there are a few rocks and numerous bright and colourful gem-stones scattered among them. These can represent particularly poignant moments, and/or important individuals. Like all Zen gardeners I observe it from the outside, from a certain height. Whenever I spot what seems to be a hard piece of stone but which is really a lump of ossified crap from my own past or personality, I try to remove it. It makes me less pompous now, but still with the potential to irritate.

So I sit on the wall looking down on the patterns I rake and often re-arrange them to help make better sense of things, while leaving a few essential rocks exactly as they are. Simplicity, simplicity… always watching out for weeds. I'll tell you about those rocks later.

In the meantime, here is the original text, interspersed with my own present musings in bold print and suitably purple prose to contrast with the grey young man I seemed to be then – with a few footnotes where needed…

# Introduction

This is a book about the Horned God. It is as relevant to women readers as it is to men. It is also about our innermost selves as they have existed in the remotest past, emerging from that past into our dire present, while seeking to evolve toward our ultimate future.

At first thought such a god exists somewhere between the designations of oddity and anachronism, and is invariably dismissed as little more than the crude focus of our even cruder ancestors. Today, in an age that is witnessing the return of the Goddess in all ways and on all levels, the idea of one more male deity may seem to be a step backward. But the Horned God is our oldest god, worshipped in light and love before humanity could even write these words. He was the true consort of that primal Goddess who is so fervently invoked as the intended cure for all our ills today. Yet when this Goddess returns to inaugurate the New Age toward which we all aspire, she will not exist in isolation. She will want her man back. In fact, she is only returning because, at long last, she can sense the Horned God, who is also the Earth God, rising to meet her as he did in the old days of her happiness. And she will not want to find that he has become a wimp.

This whole book is based upon a premise found within the field of magic – an art for which I make no apology and one for which I offer very little in the way of interpretation. It is the premise that those world-problems caused by the negative aspects of male-dominated societies can be cured not solely by reaching toward the female aspects of divinity, but also by invoking those forgotten and *positive* aspects of our most ancient god. In crude terms this is not a case of running toward Mother and asking her to stop an immature Dad being annoying, hurtful and horrible: it is matter of you meeting the old fella head-on and telling him to become greater than his present pitiful self, and become a *real* Father.

The Horned God is just, never cruel; firm but never vindictive; strong but never a bully. The Horned God loves women as equals –

one of the reasons why he was torn to pieces in the first place. He never could have imagined a world in which the feminine principle was not in perfect balance with the masculine. If the New Age is not to founder through a lack of such balance, and through a distortion of natural justice, then he must be invoked as clearly and as ardently as the Goddess who is his twin.

**I still hold to every word of that. My only quibble now is with the outdated concept of the New Age, that hairy, flarey, dawning of the 'Age of Aquarius' which we all thought was due to manifest at the Millennium. In fact, the sun will not rise in the constellation of Aquarius until May 10-11, 2437 A.D, so we are stuck with the cold flapping fish and occasionally stagnant water of Pisces for quite some time.**

**I would also add at this early stage in this new edition one vital piece of understanding: the old deities do not want our worship – the time for that sort of thing is over. They are part of us – we are part of them. There is no difference. We are the gods and goddesses, if you like. Offer respect – yes. And expect to get it back. Which might lead to a mutual sort of love. But no more bending the knee. No more veneration. The Horned God of today wants to work with us as co-equals, for that is the only way across the devastated wasteland and into the infinite growth of the forest.**

**Bear with me as I make my case about this.**

The story of the Horned God can be followed through from cave paintings in Stone Age France, along various and wondrous temples of ancient Egypt, glimpsed within the fabled halls of Camelot, and touched amid the forest depths of medieval Europe. He and his kin are also around you now, for there are gates, gaps, cracks and hidden spaces between the worlds through which we can peer at, become aware of, and occasionally step through to make contact. The more you become aware of them, the more they can engage with you.

Can modern men and women find personal relevance in such stories today? They can. In fact, we can all find something of the

••• introduction •••

Horned God's spirit within our genes. It is part of our psychological and spiritual heritage, our magical roots.

Can modern souls do anything practical about awakening the Horned God's qualities within themselves and within the world at large? They can. Intention is everything.

---

One of the advantages of age is that I have become less coy. Or perhaps the world around my internal Zen garden has become a more tolerant place than it was in my youth, more willing to observe the strange patterns of my life without screeches of laughter and scorn. So listen, the Horned God has come through to me many times in various forms and simple ways. If I use some personal anecdotes to yarn about these encounters it is to trigger off the realisation in the reader that they too will have experienced parallels, and so come to appreciate their own private Mysteries.

In his book *The White Goddess* Robert Graves played no small part in bringing the Divine Feminine back into a world whose patriarchies were rigid as metal drainpipes. But as a teenager I had been more deeply struck by an observation made in his earlier autobiography *Goodbye to All That*, which described his experiences in the First World War. He, a married man and officer in the Royal Welch Fusiliers, noted how the young soldiers queued up outside the brothels determined to lose their virginity before they were sent to almost certain death in battle. Every young man understands that impulse.

When I finally experienced sex with someone other than myself I was initiated into the act by a horny young nymph who lured me at dusk into the musky folds and forested lushness of the valley of the River Allen, in deepest Northumberland. Here on a night of full moon, around the equinox, upon the damp earth beneath the canopy of trees, she allowed me to explore her own deep folds and lush, gentle curves and – in my teenage self-image – made a man of me at last. The symbolism of the location was sublime but the sex itself made Johnny Rotten's 2 minutes and 52 seconds of squelching noises seem like a marathon. Nonetheless I was pitifully grateful; I would have gladly gone into battle then like Graves' young virgins. As for my initiatrix she never came back to me for more, but lured many another young lad into the sylvan world for delights of her own.

Yet before the act, as she led me toward the trees singing songs from the musical 'Hair' which was all the rage just then, I had the strongest feeling that Someone from another realm, omnipresent in the darkness between the trees, who knew exactly what was about to happen, was waiting. Even now, nearly 50 years later, I can recall the atmosphere but cannot find the exact way to describe that Someone other than as goat-like.

Pan, of course, although I didn't have the nous in those years to call him that. I can't pretend there was any kind of bond or sense of kinship on my part. But at various crucial moments throughout my life this Horned God appeared to me in other guises too, and we'll come to them later.

The actual construction of this book is simple. The first chapter deals with the myth of Osiris, particularly in his earliest role as both Horned God and Green Man. His family origins and marital fate are subsequently used as matrices against which we can measure and compare equally numinous myths from other Western sources. The Arthurian cultus is analysed in order to enable us to look at the same energies through a more Celtic and Anglo-Saxon focus. Aspects of the Wild Hunt, the ancient stag cults and fertility religions, plus the time-lost worship of the Divine King are also analysed in this Osirian light – not because I believe he was the first or pre-eminent Horned God, but because he was the best documented.

The primary purpose of the book is not to pass on a dry-as-dust occult history of debatable accuracy, but to awaken a sense of wonder, and to show that even the most obscure and esoteric symbols from the realm of myth can have immediate relevance to our modern lives. These myths, these 'histories' represent energies and consciousness to be found tucked away at the back of our brains. Through them we may transform ourselves without the aid of gurus, without groups and their dogmas, without that modern process of enlightenment by credit card – and without surrendering our individualities. You can do it when walking through a park. You can do it on the edge of sleep. You don't even need to think, or try to talk it through.

### ••• INTRODUCTION •••

The Horned God exists without and within. He represents a primal energy within the male and female that we scarcely have begun to acknowledge, much less tap. Call upon him and you can begin one of the most extraordinary journeys of your life.

Luck and Good Hunting to you all.

Alan Richardson
Wiltshire

# The Journey into Egypt

The magic of Egypt is older than the human mind can grasp. Dates and figures can be quoted but few people can really comprehend the spans of time involved. When the Dynastic Era began in 3150 B.C., there were deities and customs in existence whose origins were lost in the mists of time even then.

When we look toward the heart of Egypt from our cosy worlds at the start of the 21st century, our first impressions are necessarily of bewilderment: gods and goddesses as numberless as the stars; each one having several aspects; each aspect changing over the centuries, often modified by religious fads or foreign invasions. When we look into Egypt for the first time it is like looking into a child's kaleidoscope: millions of images, shifting and turning.

The only way to deal with it is to switch off the adult mind with its half-knowledge, its comparative and analytic tendencies, and take on the air of a little child who sits upon a strange and distant shore, looking out over a calm ocean with a clear mind. That way the mysterious image known as Atum can arise and – ultimately – the whole spirit of Egypt with it. Begin with that immensely simple image, and that immensely simple frame of mind, and soon the kaleidoscope will transform itself into a telescope, through which we can glimpse another world...

It began, then, with Atum, 'the Complete One,' known also as the 'Becoming One,' who was visualized as the primeval hill, or mound – the first part of the land to appear from the depths of the waters, and the place where the High God dwelled as light. Sometimes, Atum was known by the rather splendid title of 'Master of the Castle of Primeval Forms' and also as Atum-Ra. Although the scribes tended to use the

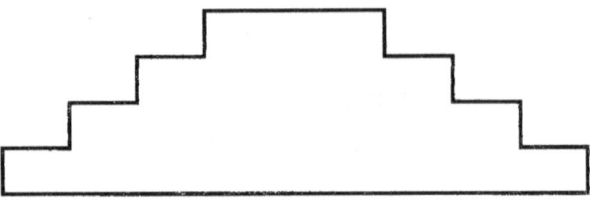

*The Primeval Mound*

masculine gender, they all knew that Atum was really bisexual – 'the Great He-She' as one text put it.

Atum appeared from nothingness. He was the first being to emerge from the absolute darkness and endless, primordial waters that existed before creation.

Becoming aware of himself he gave a great laugh and masturbated. This orgasm might be thought of as the Big Bang from which everything sprang. Really, being the only entity in the whole expanse of the infinitely empty universe, Atum had no choice but to mate with himself. And sometimes, in the desolation of our mortal lives, when we are surrounded by darkness and emptiness, it is only self-love in some form or another which can help lift us above the waters. We all know Atum.

**Yes we do. And Atum is one of the first rocks placed in my Zen garden, somewhere toward the top left-hand corner so that from where I sit and observe, there are still areas I cannot see and Mysteries remain. This is the Sacred Hill that everyone should find and explore, even if only in the mind. You can have more than one Primeval Mound in your life. They can fit into your psyche like Russian dolls. My own sacred hills are: Cley Hill, the home of a Faery King; Tan Hill that is empty of humans but packed with other revellers; Winsley Hill where I met Herne; that great chunk of rock overlooking Eilan Donan castle that seemed to be the abode of an Earth Giant; and even – at a different level – the great, conical heap of slag which once rose behind Ashington Colliery like an extinct volcano and which dominated my childhood. I expect to find more as I get older still, even though geological quirks are causing their slopes to get ever steeper each time I climb. You must all find your own. They are there in every country, every city, and every culture. If yours is**

not obviously sacred but clearly important to you, then make it sacred. The first rakings in my Zen garden all proceed from this rock.

From the seed spilled by Atum's act of self-applied sexual magic there was born the brother and sister known as Shu and Tefnut. Shu was the air and Tefnut the moisture, although the latter was sometimes also called Maat. Although these are important figures in their own right, with Mysteries enough for several lifetimes, for our present purposes we must look more closely at their offspring: Nu and Geb.

*Nu and Geb*

There are various spellings for Nu – Nuit and Nut being among the favourites. She is that elegant woman of the night sky who is pictured naked, and arched over the Earth, while beneath her is Geb, the Earth God, brother and lover, hard with desire and striving upward. He is seen kicking at the air to gain support, his member striving toward the stars and the ultimate union that he can see, smell, and anticipate until his heart almost bursts, but which he can never *quite* touch. Not in the daytime. Not in full consciousness.

We know Geb only too well, we men do. We spend lifetimes with him, seeking a grip, striving hard. And Geb knows what all men secretly know everywhere, and most invariably fight against: that Nu has the power, that hers is the strong position. Nu-woman (and new woman) comes down at her need, in the night, making dreams.

Geb is the focus of this whole book: the undisputed Earth God who would have spent eternity embracing Nu if Shu and Tefnut (acting as the earth's atmosphere) had not kept them apart during daylight. It is Geb's crown that his offspring have fought for since.

We can look at the Family Tree at this point, and try to remember.

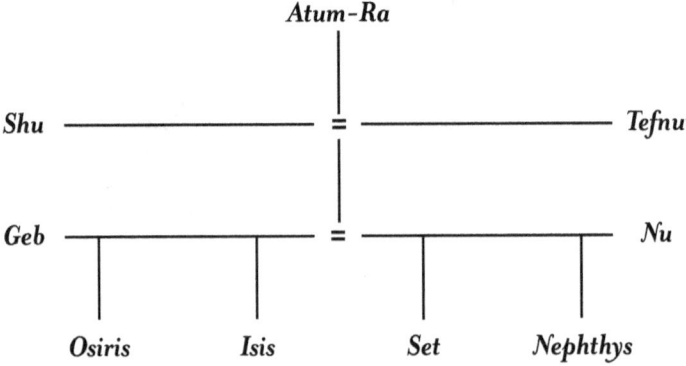

It is the children we must focus on: the two males Osiris and Set, the two females Isis and Nephthys. It was from these four souls that the majesties and miseries of the world derived. (There was a fifth, Thoth, but we need not be concerned with him yet.)

When Nu gave birth to Osiris at Thebes, a great voice was heard at the temple crying that the Lord of All was entering into the light. His names were written with the symbols of a throne and an eye, which are tentatively transcribed as As-Ar or Us-Ar. He also had many symbols ascribed to his regency: the *djed* column, which referred to his resurrection; the crook and flail by which he guided or scourged as necessary, and from which he gained the title of First Shepherd; the *atef* crown, which comprised the white crown of Upper Egypt and the two red feathers of Busiris, plus, in many depictions, the solar disk and a pair of horns. Sometimes his body was coloured red for the earth but more usually green for the vegetation.

Osiris was the first Green Man. He was clearly identified with the constellation of Orion the Hunter,[1] whom the Egyptians saw as a striding man forever looking behind him.

Osiris is immanent. He is the sufferer with all mortality but at the same time he is the power of revival and fertility in the world. He is the power of growth in plants and of reproduction in animals and human beings. He is both dead and the source of all living. To become one with Osiris is to become one with the cosmic cycles of death and rebirth...[2]

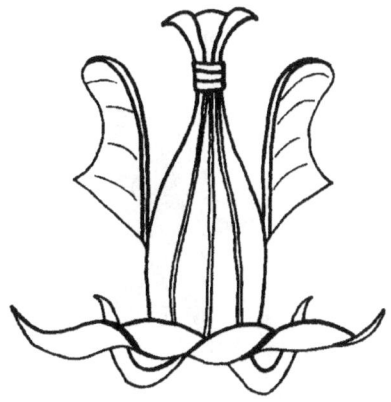

*The Atef Crown*

He was the god of the common people, supreme symbol of the life-force, 'the force that through the green fuse drives the flower' as Dylan Thomas wrote in another but apposite context. He is Geb's recognised heir, and in this sense inherits the crown of the Earth God.

In early times, accordingly, he was worshipped in 'tombs' which consisted of a tumulus in the middle of a grove. These mounds contained chambers which were reached by winding passages. Here, in the Underworld, the seeker could commune with Osiris.

The details intimidate at first. A strange god worshipped at weird altars. And what woman has never crawled into a lonely bed, sinking down into labyrinths of despair, following the endless turnings of a ravaged heart to try to reach that one, pure image within – to try to reach man as he should be but never is: a man wrapped like a gift and shiny-new, a present for the woman alone, the first love and true love who, at the core, can never fade, and must never decay. What woman has never reached toward that Osirian spark within her son, lover, husband, or father? The woman hasn't been born who has never worshipped this strange god at those weird altars. They search for him constantly, in all of his parts.

---

1  Yet Philip Coppens argues convincingly in *The Canopus Revelation* that it is the star Canopus that was linked with Osiris, not Orion.
2  R. T. Rundle Clark, *Myth and Symbol in Ancient Egypt*. (London: Thames and Hudson, 1959), p. 97

Then there is his twin, Isis, with whom he fell in love when still in Nu's womb. She became perhaps the most enduring and dominant of all the figures within the Egyptian pantheon, her worship lasting for thousands of years and spreading throughout the Mediterranean world and beyond.

*Osiris bearing the crook, flail, and uas wand*

As his twin, Isis shares part of his name: As-t, more simply Ast, or even Aset, which means a throne or a seat. She taught Osiris the practice of agriculture, gave mankind the arts of medicine, instituted marriage in the World, taught women the domestic arts of corn-grinding, flax-spinning and weaving, and generally functioned as the Great Enchantress, mistress of all the magic under the Moon. In later versions of her image she can be seen with the child, the infant Horus: she wears on her head a disk set between the horns of a cow, and she was often identified with Hathor (my own favourite goddess) who came from elsewhere.

This often happens to Great Goddesses: their single nature becomes like a crystal lens: shafted by the light of man's perception, it breaks up on the other side into a complete spectrum of goddesses. But her unified symbol in the heavens was unquestionably the star Sirius, which they knew as Sothis.

The appearance of this star marked the beginning of a new year and announced the advance of the Inundation of the Nile. We can find her, and hear all of Egypt's voice, in the cry of all tiny children at play: 'Mummy's coming, Mummy's coming – quick! quick!' This is because the safe terror and the happy fear as she strides into their little games echoes exactly the voices along the Nile, when Sothis rose, bringing the waters.

Isis endures. That is her power. Through all the coming and going of men who become friends, lovers, husbands, and then become like little children again themselves – through all the bitter delights of having children who first adore, and then scorn and then love again, when they mature – she endures. She holds things together as thrones can, when properly used. As a throne she bears weight, the kingly burdens of life. She is the one constant thing. As a throne, an empty throne, she is that which can take our weight, whose arms can offer us rest and protection. She wraps around us when we place the burdens of our bodies upon her, and in doing so we feel like kings and queens ourselves.

Isis is special, and makes us feel special. But she was chiefly worshipped for the part she played after the death of Osiris. Then she really came into her own.

Osiris was in fact murdered, which is probably the only good way for a god to die. Death by murder produces far more reverberations than the quiet decrepitude of age. The Osirian reverberations can still be felt.

The culprit was his twin brother Set, who had always hated him. Set indeed believed that he should have been Geb's heir. And every time that Set looked upon his brother and saw how good, beautiful, perfect and beloved he was, he grew angry. We have all been in Set's place, too. We have all looked out through his mask. So it happened that Set invited Osiris to a banquet, a kind of 'Last Supper' in which a gorgeous chest was brought out, and the offer made that whoever fit inside it perfectly could have it. The chest was illuminated with suns and stars, inlaid with precious jewels so that it looked like a model of the heavens themselves – not the anaemic dots of light that we perceive above the neon polluted skies of our present world, but the staggering intensity of the ancient night when you could almost hear the music of the spheres and the sound of the wind through space, rushing between the worlds.

Now Osiris was so good, so nice, that he loved and trusted his brother, and needed no second bidding to lie down within the chest, which fitted him perfectly. No sooner had he done so than Set and his 70 companions pounced on and trapped him inside. The number is so specific that some scholars have seen the whole Set/Osiris/Horus rivalry as coded imagery describing astronomical alignments and changes that I cannot begin to understand. The differing interpretations are not in any way incompatible when you accept the dictum As Above, So Below.

Eventually, as the story goes, the coffin was washed ashore in Byblos, in Syria, where it became ensnared in the branches of a tamarisk tree which enclosed the coffin completely in its trunk. The tree in turn was cut down and taken to form a pillar in the palace of the King of Syria. This is one of the things represented by the *djed* column.

Meanwhile Isis, using her magic, traced the coffin to the palace. Disguised as an old nursemaid the mask accidentally slipped one night and the King of Syria, awed by her greatness, granted her the pillar which contained the coffin. Who could refuse Isis? Who could deny a goddess?

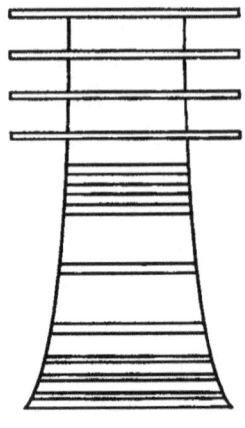

*The djed column*

Triumphant, she returned home with the coffin and hid it on the isle of Chemmis in the Delta. But as ill luck would have it, Set and his 70 companions found the coffin and tore it open. They then ripped Osiris' body into 14 pieces which were then scattered over the length and breadth of Egypt. That, felt Set, was the only way to treat someone like Osiris. And Set was right, though for the wrong reasons.

Isis search began in earnest then. She set out with her nephew Anubis (of whom more later) to find each piece. This was no problem for Anubis, the black dog or jackal who can sniff between the worlds. In some versions whenever she found a piece she buried it with due honours – thus accounting for the many 'burial places' of Osiris all over Egypt. In other versions she uses her magic to reassemble him. And what modern woman has never, even if only occasionally, craved the power to be able to do that to her husband – to reassemble him in the way that she wants? All agree that there was one piece of her husband's body – the phallus – which she did not find: it had been cast into the Nile and eaten by a fish, which Isis promptly cursed.

Undeterred, she used her powers to create a replica either of gold or wood, which was every bit as potent as the real thing. From this magic dildo, Horus was conceived. We will look more closely at him later, too.

Horus was raised by his mother and his aunt, Nephthys. He was taught how to fight, with all the berserker fury that only women can express, if they want. Despite being something of a cripple at birth – he was very weak from the waist down – he nevertheless grew strong, preparing himself daily until the time came when he would challenge his uncle for the Earth God's crown. In due course, after a mighty combat and much litigation in the courts of the gods, Horus triumphed.

And it is here that we find ourselves at a crucial juncture of our consciousness, for although Osiris could have reclaimed his throne, he preferred to maintain his kingdom in the Land of the Dead, and it was thus as God of the Dead that Osiris enjoyed his greatest popularity. Among other things, Osiris had learned that most difficult secret which many sons, lovers, husbands, and fathers never learn: when to hold, and when to let go. Osiris let go, and granted Horus the Earth God's crown. He set Isis free in other ways, too.

**Everyone reading this will at some point in their life have known what it is like to have been torn apart, roughly re-assembled but missing something, finding themselves existing in a horrible state of limbo, scarcely able to move, paralysed. This is a parallel of Osiris in the Underworld.**

**In one of the versions of the myth, the latter was able to energise himself again by calling for the help of his twin sisters Isis and Nephthys: 'Come to me quickly!' or *sj.k rj.* was his cry. Thus was the name Skr or Sokaris created. The very moment he did this he gained wings, he started to soar – he became Horus the Hawk with a glimpse of new horizons.**

**When we are alone and trapped in our private dead zone we can voice our own internal Call, one which will motivate ourselves, drag us out of stasis and help us motivate ourselves again. The Call is a simple one, uttered with self-directed anger, personal exasperation, soaring new determination, and can be vocalised as something like: Oh for Fuck's Sake – *Live!***

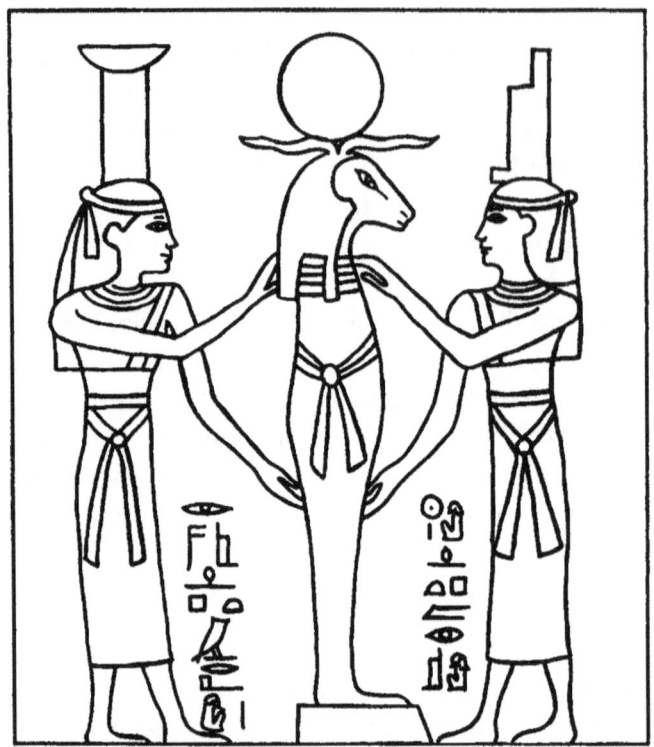

*Osiris and Ra as one god, sustained by Nephthys and Isis*

Osiris' kingdom was supposed to be beneath Nun, also called 'Infinity, Nothingness, Nowhere, and Darkness,' or in the Northern heavens, or else in the West. It is reminiscent of Western magical concepts of Atlantis. To the British mind this was in the West, and to the magicians of Germany to the North. The Kingdom of the Dead in the ancient world, however, was not some dread and dark place, but one of light and love. In a world of short lives and sudden death, it was the place where old loves could be renewed – not just for the fraught years of the mortal realm, but for the millions and millions of years of the Egyptian ideal. It was from the dead, who were usually buried in family and ancestral groupings at the edge of the desert (symbolic in itself) that a person's temporal power and wisdom was derived.

It was Osiris who helped mediate these divine energies between the Underworld and this world. Every man in Egypt became an Osiris at death, not only for theological reasons but because it was as the First Love that he was always recalled, never in his ultimate geriatric form.

And his *ka*, too, assumed that early vigorous shape of the deceased in his prime that souls will always assume in the immediate after-death states.

**There is nothing too bizarre about that last. William G. Gray told me that when his father's spirit first returned he didn't recognise him, as he came back as a young man. Today, as I work with old people as part of my job, I know they all feel themselves to be teenagers inside, and that is how they will re-appear to me. When I pass on I will make a brief spirit return as a 22-year-old hunk, doing one-handed push-ups.**

And that, in brief, is the story of Osiris. A story which continues today, ever-becoming. Nothing will ever change, or stop, until the world returns to the pre-Atum realm of Nun, to 'Infinity, Nothing, Nowhere, and Darkness,' as happens to all worlds eventually. But in our case it will happen sooner rather than later, unless we can learn to balance the gods within us.

**Another advantage of the Zen garden is that I can pattern it how I want. I sit here rather pompously holding my rake like some Egyptian deity with his *uas* wand and occasionally use it to make patterns curve out from the Atum-rock that holds my essence. But I pause now, struck by that sentence above: 'Nothing will ever change, or stop, until the world returns to Nun, to Infinity, Nothing, Nowhere, and Darkness, as happens to all worlds eventually.' There are times in everyone's life when the constant raking gets you nowhere and explains nothing, and creates no more than dark, aimless furrows caused by the sharp tines of thought rasping through dead material.**

    **I think this is what Basilides meant when he wrote about Ignorance and Silence. My only grasp of languages are in English, British Sign Language, Geordie and Schoolboy French, but I feel that a better translation of 'Ignorance' would be Not-Knowing, which of course takes us into modern perceptions of Zen awareness.**

Sometimes you have to rake it all flat again, wipe out the patterns, stop all conscious thought, all internal monologues and analyses, and simply listen to your breath, becoming like a creature in a forest. When I first started invoking the Earth God – be it Geb, Osiris, Pan, Herne, Cernunnos – it was not through physical rituals involving written and spoken invocations, but via simple nothingness and silence. A number of my work mates in those days thought that I was a bit thick. I was certainly irritating.

These essential elements from the Osirian Cycle have been taken from the Heliopolitan version, which is the nearest thing to an orthodoxy that the whole of Egyptian Mythology possesses. Like any orthodoxy, and like the Bible, we can take images and quotations to support almost any proposition that we care to make. This, after all, is the whole purpose of myth. We stride through the apparent chaos of symbols and perform what magic we can to make those glyphs come alive which best respond to our own natures. In so doing, they can in turn make us come alive.

By taking the bare bones of the Osirian myth, and assembling them to our own delight, we begin to assemble something wondrous within ourselves. The more we interpret and relate, the more we put veins and sinews and muscle-tissue upon the skeleton and find ourselves able to live life in a differing way, using new muscles of our own. All of it, no matter how trivial, how absurd, goes toward making Osiris live again, and bringing life to ourselves.

Isis would like that.

**The fellow who wrote the above, and what follows, is absolutely right but he does go on a bit, clearly likes the sound of his own voice and is probably trying a bit too hard to write beautiful prose. If I were to meet him now, I'm not sure we'd get on. I think I'd find him boring. He's not coming anywhere near this new garden of mine and he's certainly not touching my lovely three-tined rake.**

Someone once said that only through children can we achieve immortality. While we might debate the truth of this statement, we can at least applaud the warmth behind it. Whoever said it, male or female, would certainly have loved Isis. No woman before or since has ever loved her husband, or her husband's children, as much as she did.

As we have seen, her child by her brother Osiris was known as Horus. This is the Latinized form of the Egyptian Hor, or Heru. One of the earliest forms of Horus was Haroeris (or Harwer), derived from a combination of the Falcon God with the deity *Wer*, 'the Great One,' a serpent of light whose eyes were the Sun and Moon.

When Isis knew that she was pregnant with the seed of her brother Osiris her heart rejoiced. To her mind Horus would, when born, become something of a wonder-child, a saviour – not only for the world at large, but also for his father in the Underworld. Horus would bring light and love upon the earth, and the certainty of new beginnings. He would subdue those malicious forces represented by Set. Through him, in his falcon form, mankind would soar. This is the Great One, *Wer*, the serpent of light – but with wings – wings made from the feathers of Maat. This is the Earth God who has learned that formula whereby he can rise up toward the stars, instead of waiting for them to come down to him. It is a formula that derives from the serpent energies within the earth and within ourselves.

This is the kundalini of Indian Tantrism. Horus, as his mother knew well, was and always will be the 'sign of something coming.' He is also Hope, that last creature within Pandora's Box, and the silver lining on every cloud. When things are bleak, Horus' hawk-head is that which we can see hovering in the distance.

As a child, brought up in secrecy on the floating island of Chemmis, in the marshes near Buto, he was known as Harpokrates, 'the infant Horus.' He was weakly and stunted from the waist down – perhaps because his father was dead when the child was conceived. During all his battles with Set to claim the Earth God's crown, the land itself suffered dreadfully. It became a Wasteland. The crucial moment occurs when the triumphant son claims admission to his father's house in the Underworld, saying:

> Tell him that I have come hither to save
> myself and enliven my two cobras (eyes),

> to sit in the room of Father Osiris
> and to dispel the sickness of the suffering god,
> so that I can appear an Osiris in strength,
> that I may be reborn with him in his renewed vigour,
> that I may reveal to you the matter of Osiris' thigh
> and read to you from that sealed roll which lies beneath his side,
> whereby the mouths of the gods are opened.³

Horus, as the King's heir and outer representative, is there to cure a mysterious wound in the thigh – a euphemism for the genitals – so that life will gush forth upon the land again. In order to cure Osiris fully, another version of the myth has Horus ask his father what ails him, in a manner that exactly parallels the question which had to be asked of the Fisher King in Arthurian mythology. The latter, ruler of a wasteland and keeper of the Holy Grail, suffered the same 'wound in the thigh' as Osiris. In both cases, once the question is put, the wound heals, life gushes forth upon the land again, and Maat, order, is restored.

Perhaps Maat will make more sense if we think of her as representing the Balance of Nature, for this is closer to the meaning of Maat than the concepts of Order, or Truth, that commonly have been used up until now. We will deal with the Holy Grail, and that mysterious 'roll' concealed within Osiris' side in later chapters.

There is another secret concealed within the interchange of energies and consciousness between Horus and Osiris. It is simply that Osiris must set himself in motion and transcend his own helplessness. Horus can only do so much. The whole meeting between the victorious son and his paralyzed father is really an uncompromising exhortation to self-reliance. Once this attitude has been achieved within Osiris, and Horus has performed the mysterious ceremony known as the 'Opening of the Mouth,' using an adze which represents the constellation of the Great Bear (belonging to Set), the balance between the worlds then is truly restored, the inner and outer worlds fertile again. All of this can be restated in very simple terms:

*We need Osiris. Osiris needs us.*
*We need the Land. The Land needs us.*

---

3  Ibid., Coffin Text No. 228.

Redemption has always been a two-way process, whatever the mystery.

Much of this is made more comprehensible in the light of Maat. She is the feather-like touch of gnosis, the balance between the opposites: Upper and Lower Egypt; the fertile valley and the desert; good and evil, and so on. She was the very basis of civilisation and the true source of Egypt's strength, and was perhaps the earliest attempt to express the concept of Mother Nature – not simply in the sense of a green world teeming with life, but as a world existing and thriving through a divine and perfect order. Maat teaches us all we know about ecology and ecosystems, food chains, natural cycles, and all those often invisible patterns of life and death which influence us all.

She was to be found within the Judgment Hall of Osiris, into which she ushered the soul of the deceased. Her feather was then placed in one pan of the balance while the heart of the deceased was placed in the other. If the scales balanced, the heart was said to be 'justified,' and 'true of voice.' It thus fitted into its allotted place in the divine order – which was also the natural order of the world. Horus, then, put the world to rights by revivifying the inner kingdom of Osiris, and that outer kingdom which he now ruled himself.

Set, meanwhile, had been brought in chains before the gods. They only spared him on the condition that, as god of the wind and storms, he would convey the boat of Osiris through the Underworld. Well, he had little choice, really. Poor old Set – it was only through

*The goddess Maat*

his imperfections that Osiris' faultless nature was given any meaning. How can we measure 'goodness' unless we have a yardstick of 'badness' to measure it by? It was Set who made the gods god-like. As the worst among us, he should be given the best of our love; but that is an arcanum that humanity is not yet ready or willing to achieve.

How embarrassing. That last sentence makes it sound as if I, personally, had balanced my heart with the feather of Maat in the Judgement Hall many times, and was some distance ahead of humanity with respect to giving love to Set. That young man was being pompous, pretentious and portentous. In truth, at that time, there were huge areas of life in which he just did not have a clue. His heart would have been so heavy in the scales that the feather of Maat would have been catapulted to the high ceilings of the Judgement Hall.

Mind you, it was Carl Jung who said that when the archetypes first speak they are always pompous, so I will take heart from that. Jung's stock among today's psychotherapists has fallen so low that he is often referred to as the Madame Blavatsky of the movement. I would disagree: he was the MacGregor Mathers of early psychotherapy, an out-and-out magus who had to hide his true impulses behind a veneer of 'science'. In fact he believed that he was an avatar or incarnation of the Gnostic deity Aion, and I think he probably was.[4]

Pomposity apart, whether from me or from the gods, the fact is, Set *has* had a raw deal. It was the late and great Billie Walker-John and our magical artist pal Judith Page who approached me with the idea of doing an *Inner Guide to Set*, although it came to nothing. To them Osiris was a late-comer and Judith in her uncompromising Australian way always referred to him as the Dickless Wonder.

Long, long ago before there was an Ancient Egypt as we know it, there was a prehistoric proto-kingdom in what is now Southern or Upper Egypt called Nubt, of which Set was the ruling deity. Set the Golden. Set the Mighty. Set of Nubt. This was the one Billie and Judith had picked up, not the whipping boy for Osiris.

---

4 See Richard Noll's excellent *The Aryan Christ* for detailed insight into this hidden (but very obvious) aspect of an extraordinary man. Ignore the pissy reviews on Amazon by those who were frightened of Jung's occult and volkisch side and make up your own mind.

··· the journey into egypt ···

Any serious study of Egypt inevitably unearths fragments of worship from times when Set was *the* deity of choice for the common folk, long before the usurper Osiris came on the scene. They worshipped him not because they feared his power, but perhaps because they understood the qualities of Night and Darkness better than we do today.

I came to do a lot of solitary work with Set over the years for he is an Earth God too, in differing ways, and I have always found him pure and true. His 70 Companions were described as just about every 'evil' or dangerous animal and creature known to Egypt: hippopotamus, pig, donkey, crocodile, scorpion, turtle and many more. Which indicates that Set had every right (and rite) to be regarded as an heir to Geb too, every bit the equal of his twin brother. An Egyptian version of Pan, perhaps? Or of Cernunnos, the Lord of Animals?

When he wasn't wearing his theriomorphic mask he was believed to have white skin and red hair, with the Egyptians comparing his hair to the pelt of a donkey – another of his symbols. Red animals and even people with red hair were thought to be his followers. These animals were sometimes sacrificed, while the link between Set and red-heads – usually foreigners – was seen to give him godhood over foreign lands but leave him marked as the perpetual Outsider.

As the Lord of Darkness (to give him another title) Set has been reviled and feared for thousands of years. Everything that ever went wrong, every nasty, cruel, depraved and vicious act was seen as having the hallmark of Set. In time, by juggling about with name-origins and quasi-histories, Set the Lord of Darkness came to be seen as the prototype of Satan, the very Prince of Darkness, and thus the root of all evil. Like Pan and Cernunnos in fact.

I would argue that over the aeons a distortion crept into the way we look at the binaries of existence:

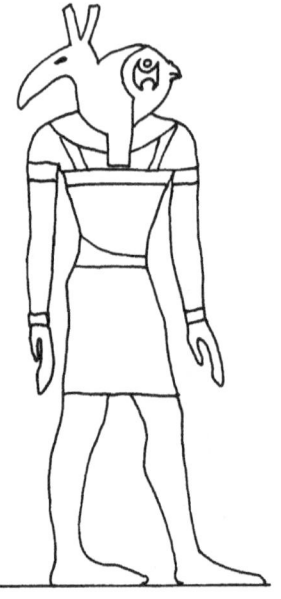

Horus/Set
Order/Chaos
Light/Darkness
Positive/Negative
Day/Night
Life/Death

... and so on. The distortion came through adding Good/Evil to this list. Thus the qualities of Darkness, Chaos, Night and so forth, were all seen as expressions of Set and so linked with the quality of Evil. This was never an aspect of Set's original nature, for the Lord of Darkness is an inseparable partner to the Lord of Light.

There is even an inelegant but little known image of a deity bearing the heads of both Horus and Set and this should be the ideal: Light and Darkness in balance.

The most Ancient Egyptians gave no moral dimensions to Set's role in their earliest Mysteries.

However it is possible to learn how to work within the heart of Set's darkness. Those shadows caused by the wall of my Zen garden, and the rocks, and even the tiny shadings caused by the myriad pebbles, enable us to find our way to those sources of light which actually cause these, and are part of this Alternative Earth God's own Mystery. In short, Darkness is a necessary corollary to the Light; Shadow is a means of defining existence; those magics of the Dark and Night have nothing to do with Evil and everything to do with balance, renewal and – surprisingly – healing.

This is not a question of inverting morality and taking the crass stance of 'Evil be thou my Good'. Or of trying to win through to purity by indulging our atavistic urges and then conquering them. And even less does it relate to summoning depraved entities from the pit of our subconscious. Dire warnings have always been given out to those who have wanted to invoke Set. Yet in almost all cases the would-be summoner is moved by entirely the wrong impulse – while those giving the warning are invariably ignorant of the true nature of Set's energies.

So what I can say now, sitting on the low wall of age and reminiscence and twiddling my rake is this:

If you work with Set, then the first thing you might experience is Chaos. Your world could be shaken and turned inside-out. Everything might seem to fall apart. In practice Set usually comes to the fringes of the psyche when there is no other spiritual option, and he becomes that energy which can break chains, smash down barriers, and set you free...

Judith's description of Osiris as the Dickless Wonder, while being rich in chuckleness, gives a refreshing and powerful antidote to those who try to fit the Green One into yet another orthodoxy that we all must follow – or else. When you find your own way in life, be aware that there is always Another Path that will get you to the same place in the end.

I suspect we'll come back to Set later. In the meantime, let's see what that young fella is burbling about now...

His heritage now restored, Horus was declared ruler of the two Egypts, and titled *Har-pa-Neb-Taui*, 'Horus, Lord of the Two Lands.' This was a title later echoed by the pharaohs themselves, who all took the name Horus as one of their own. This reminds us of the long practice (now ceased) of giving male heirs to the throne of the British Royal Family the name of Arthur somewhere in their long list of first names. Then began the long but happy process of rebuilding all those temples of his ancestors which Set had destroyed. Then began another Age within the world.

We who stand here on the polluted shores of the Piscean Age, watching the waters ebbing away with the final years of this century, can see the fishes themselves giving their last gasps in the strange atmospheres that are now being revealed to them. We can, with some delight and awe, and no little fear, watch Horus swoop down upon the last years of this era to pluck up one of those fishes within his talons. The death of the Piscean Age is hastened as he feeds upon it and builds up his own strength, absorbing the creature's power as an Aztec warrior would consume his enemy's heart. The fish itself contains the debris of our own wearied civilizations. But it also contains that long lost phallus of Osiris. And to help us leave the realms of simple myth and enter those of magical prophecy even further, we must now consider the nature of that other son: We must now consider Anubis.

I stumbled upon Anubis without realising it. This was probably around 1981, in a cobbled back-street in Bath. A tiny little spiritualist medium with a marked limp, a Mrs Butler from Weston-super-Mare, told me of two beings who were floating around me, one named Bert and the other with rather a difficult name, somewhat like Yvonne or Yvette or something.

She was spot on. The first was my private name for David Herbert Lawrence who had bothered me and buggered me up as a writer for many years. The second was clearly that of Ywi, or Yvius, a Celtic monk from 7th Century Lindisfarne who had been causing all sorts of ructions and synchronicities in my inner and outer life.

But then she added: 'I also see a black dog around you. Does this mean anything?' It did not. I have never had a dog and never will. Don't like them. 'It's big and black with high pointed ears.' Still it did not register. 'It is part of you and in some sense it is you ... Bear this in mind, will you?'

Bert and Ywi meant everything, the black dog nothing. It was only a week later when I met Dolores Ashcroft-Nowicki for the first time, and asked her about the inner contact of her Servants of Light group that she told me: Anubis. When I told her what Mrs Butler had said, and my bewilderment, she commented: 'Ha ha my boy ... you've been shepherded.' The critter leapt into my head and life and taught me all sorts of things from that moment on.

Dolores is one of the gem-stones that I have placed amid the otherwise featureless pebbles of my garden. This one is large, and turquoise and glowing. She and Anubis triggered off powerful events in my life and the first edition of *Earth God Rising* was largely inspired by their contact.

I met the wildwood wizard Dusty Miller that day too, who gave me two elf-wands that are still among my most treasured possessions, but that's another story. He can have a gem-stone too.

To understand the Anubis, however, we must first look at his mother, Nephthys. Gods are no different to us in this respect. Nephthys was Nu's second daughter, and although she was married to Set, her love and passion was for Osiris. As wife to the god of aridity and tempest, she conceived no children to make her own life happier. So in despair she disguised herself as her sister, Isis, in order to sleep with her true love. The result of this union was Anubis. (The more purely Egyptian form of the name is Anpu.)

If Isis is the woman who endures, Nephthys is the one who survives. We see the best of her in the single parent who will bring up her children despite all the odds, and who has still got something left over for herself. We see her in the sort of woman who has the chameleon powers to blend into any background, for any purpose, or else who becomes an active shape-shifter – able to become, on the surface, whatever people want her to be, while retaining an inner spark that is unique and unquenchable. Isis *is*, to make a word-play, but Nephthys constantly mirrors change.

Her son, Anpu, was a fine son, the sort any goddess would be proud to have. Seeing him as a dog or jackal-deity, the Egyptians naturally associated him with the western desert, or the home of the dead. In some early sources he took over the title of the funerary god Khenti-Amentiu, 'First of the Westerners.' Another of his titles, in his full jackal form of Wepwawet, was 'Opener of the Way.' This is the title we must eventually fasten upon.

Anpu had a humour as black as his skin, though not without compassion, and an insight as bleak as the desert he haunted, though it was not without luminosity. He had – and has – all the power and blackness of a person who has long since mastered the self-destructive urges within him and can now see the possibilities of mastering his own fate. As alert as his sharp ears indicate, he can hear things coming from hundreds of miles and thousands of years away. His memory, activated by his extraordinary sense of smell, reaches the full circle of forgotten past and unimagined future. Capable of cruelty, he yet became the Guardian of women and small children. He is his mother's son all right, but with a touch of Set in him somewhere.

Fearing Set's vengeance when he found out about her treachery, Nephthys exposed her infant as soon as he was born, casting him adrift into the marshes – an act which she regretted instantly and so intensely that she fled and confessed everything to Isis. Her sister was

*Anubis – **Opener of the Way***

then able to find the baby Anubis during her own searches for Osiris. She adopted him and loved him as her own. This sounds as if it might be a casual enough piece of the story, or a mere linkage between the major episodes, but there is more to it than that. As we will see later, everyone who searches for Osiris, and what he represents, stumbles upon Anubis first.

After this supreme act of sisterly love and intense jealousy on Isis' part, Nephthys joined her in all her trials. Together they found the body of Osiris. As kites, great long-winged birds of the falcon family, they mourned over his corpse. At times we can still hear them: the two voices within a woman at the breakdown of a marriage which say: *I'm going to take this from him, take everything, so that he won't leave me* – that is the thin voice of the diminutive Isis; and then: *I'll give the bastard hell, that way he won't do it again* – that is Nephthys in her rage.

These are not the goddess voices in full power, but instead voices heard distantly, down a long, long tube.

In early times Anubis was something of a Death God for the pharaoh alone – a sacred executioner, a masked Priest of Anubis, who would ritually murder the pharaoh by means of a viper at the end of a stipulated time.

Of all the other images discussed so far, remember that one. We will come back to it in some detail in later chapters.

In his role as Lord of Magic, Anubis could see the past and future with ridiculous ease. In fact he was the past and future, for he also came to be described as Time. In the role of Time, the Devourer, he is described as devouring the Apis Bull, one of the major symbols of Osiris himself, who was often known as Kai Imentet, the 'Bull of the West.'

Another symbol of his was a black and white ox-hide spattered with blood and hanging from a pole. And if we look closely at the large and upward-pointing ears, we will see that we are not that far from the Horned God who is central to our thesis.

Most representations tend to show Anubis as a jackal-headed man, although this has sometimes been interpreted as a dog: whence the dog-headed Hermes in that mythology which the Greeks borrowed from Egypt. Sometimes he is shown accompanying Isis – an allusion to his role and title as Guardian. Small statuettes of him were kept by Egyptian bedsides to guard over people's dreams, while even today magicians have been known to invoke his image and use it to protect properties, or else set him and his astral hounds loose beyond the peripheries of those circles within which they perform their Work.

Anubis was regarded as being identical to Osiris himself in many sources. At some centres, such as Oxyrhynchus and Cynopolis, the two were identical. It was E. A. Wallis Budge, the legendary Egyptologist and translator of the Book of the Dead, who speculated that the cult of Anubis was perhaps the most ancient of all, and that in some ways the Osirian Cult actually was consumed by that of the jackal. He wrote:

> Others again are of the opinion that by Anubis is meant Time, and that his denomination of Kuon [the Greek word for 'dog'] does not so much allude to any likeness, which he has to the dog ... as to that other signification of the term taken from breeding; because Time begets all things out of it self, bearing them within itself, as it were in a womb.[5]

We can also associate him with the number 9. Multiply any number by 9, e.g. 9 x 13 = 117. Add the digits of the answer – 1 + 1 + 7 – and you get 9 again. This is Anubis doing in the world of Number what he does within our genes.

Apart from his relationship to, and identification with, Osiris, the god Anubis also functions as the Dark Twin in tandem with Horus as the Bright Twin. Even though these are roles taken from the mythological structures of megalithic Europe, they are still valid in this context. Anubis, who was conceived while Osiris was still 'in the flesh,' finds himself a creature of the Earth, linked with the natural cycles as Time itself. Horus, who was conceived after his father's death, is more a creature of Fire and Air, swooping down from heights. And although it was the Hawk who inherited the kingship from Osiris, it will be Anubis, the Dark Twin and Sacrificial Priest, who will bring this kingship to an end, spill blood upon the land, and give life to the world anew.

That might not be clear yet, but it will be.

Here is a prophecy to go with it:

Soon, a woman will conceive by inseminating herself with the frozen sperm of her dead husband. The child, a boy, will have

---

5  E. A. Wallis Budge, *The Gods of the Egyptians* (London: Routledge and Kegan Paul, 1904), Vol. II, pp. 264-265. Budge was long rumoured to have been linked with a magical group which met in the basement of the British Museum, using the Egyptian artifacts there as the basis for their temple.

something wrong with his legs at first. But after intense treatment, paid for by his aunt, he will become almost as mobile as any child, except for a slight limp he will have for all of his short life. The boy, inheriting his father's talents, will set the world and the hearts of women alight …

I'll stand by that, though I doubt if I'll ever know of its fulfilment. I had a lot of wobbly clairvoyant bursts in those days (none now) which were usually accurate.

However, when I was writing my dual biography *Aleister Crowley and Dion Fortune*, I came across a notion by Timothy Leary which struck me as apposite. He felt that the universe has innumerable 'scripts' for which we provide the actors. Every person reading this, therefore, will at some point re-enact one or more of the great mythic scripts. It does not mean they are avatars or reincarnations of the figures involved, but 'continuations'.

So however modest, small, unimportant or trivial you might feel your own life is, be assured that at all times you understudy the gods and step up into their roles without realising it. Modern scientists, gripped by the potentials of the Quantum Universe, tell us (using the same terms of the mystics they scorned of old) that everything which can happen does happen, and that we are all connected.

Not so much As Above so Below, but more a case of As Without, So Within...

This, so far, has been a fairly exoteric introduction to the standard myths relating to the particular figures. The purist might quibble that no reference has been made to other versions of this mythology, or to major figures such as Horus the Elder, Thoth, Ptah, Sekhmet, or the enigmatic and important Benu Bird, who is seen at the Beginning and the End of Time. Indeed the list of omissions is endless, the areas of overlap and interaction almost infinite. Still, no apology can, should, or will be made; persons must find their own myths and work them through. That is what they are for. They are to initiate people. In the strictest sense of the word, myths are there to help them 'begin.' This beginning is everything – far more important than purity or accuracy of scholarship, far more vital than a correct assembly of all the scholarly facts. As soon as people begin to work with their myths – however crudely – the myths begin to work with them. They become Initiates from then on.

So we must now strike an attitude and play a game. There is no need to go back over the earlier details to try to fully remember and comprehend everything – at least not yet. The vital work is already being done by the subconscious, in that sort of subliminal brooding which will eventually produce surface results.

First, we must adopt that childlike but not childish attitude in which we can approach the Heliopolitan Recension with all the wonder, awe, and delight that we once reserved for our favourite fairy-tales. In doing this, we must realize that each part is vital to the whole, and resist the adult temptation to isolate and analyse and invariably venerate. Who cares, when they are three years old, what Snow White can symbolize? Or that great sociological commentaries can be found within the names of the dwarfs ... The important thing is what they did, and how. Similarly Isis cannot be considered without her consort, nor Anpu without his mother. This is not sexism, but balance, for the gods are part of us, and the parts must function properly.

Basically, we must try to relate the functions of the gods (as we understand them) to mundane items of daily life.

Take a torch for example. Osiris is the battery, Horus is the bulb, Nephthys the switch, Anubis those fittings which conduct the circuit of electricity, Isis the case which contains them all – and Set the darkness which creates the torch's very purpose.

Or: Osiris is the seed, Isis the soil, Horus the sun which brings the growth.

Or: Osiris is the petrol, Isis the ignition chamber, Horus the ignition spark – and Set the exhaust gases.

Or: Anything, really. It is a game that you can only win, there can be no losers. In a very real sense it begins to awaken the gods within the world, and therefore within the magician's own consciousness.

In time the Opener of the Way himself will come to help.

There is one final concept that we must consider before continuing. It is the nature of the Underworld in which Osiris chose to remain, known to Egyptians as *Dat, Duat* or even *Tuat*, pronounced exactly like the English vulgarism 'twat'. Although this concept has been ignored or minimised, it actually provides each magical tradition with its real sources of power and endurance.

To the Egyptians, death and life were different sides of the same door. One was meaningless, without the other. The Underworld was where things were given the shape and form in which they would later appear within this World. It is the astral plane, and the subconscious mind.

Despite the convenient term 'Underworld,' the Tuat was in fact given no specific location. Most often it was regarded as being under the Earth, but it was sometimes regarded as being beyond the vault of the stars – or else in those Waters that they imagined extended everywhere beneath the land.

The symbol for the Underworld was ⊗

While the symbol for the stars was ✶

Not a great deal of difference there. 'It is the place of the formation of the living out of the dead and the past, the true meeting-place of time before and after.' Its gates were protected by fire-spitting serpents, lions, or dragons, and by a sphinx-like creature known as the Aker, which held the Eastern and Western portals. It is therefore the place of the ancestors, of souls long dead and yet waiting to be born. In some senses it is the cerebellum, containing all our racial memories, and in others it is the womb. The symbol for the star, which so temptingly asks to be transformed into the pentagram beloved of modern occultists, should perhaps be regarded more like a sphincter which is capable of being pushed, peeled, or pried open.

Through that narrow entrance is the Underworld. It is the opened cervix leading to the womb. The Tuat, and the twat, is the means by which we can give birth to ourselves.

# And Then Camelot

All myths are living energies. The ones in question were ancient when the First Dynasty began around 3100 B.C. – and yet they are no age at all. They are instead ever-becoming, like the spurting of Atum, or the column of some sparkling and infinite fountain. How to find that fountain, and when to drink from it, is something that we can spend a lifetime studying only to find (as seekers always do) that it is within us all along.

One of those figures from the realms of myth and history who was more aware of such matters than most was a certain priest from the 26th Dynasty. Now he knew all about this sort of thing, as he never ceased to tell anyone who cared to listen. Many of the people thought him insufferable because of this, but the man had absolute conviction as to his merit and his destiny, and he never ceased to prophesy. That was what he was best at.

His name was Ankh-f-n-Khonsu, which means 'His heart is with Khonsu.' Khonsu was the old Moon God from Thebes, where the mysteries functioned on a more subconscious level than elsewhere. This Dynasty, which ran from 663 to 525 B.C. – as near as such things can be determined – saw pharaohs bearing the names Necho and Psamtik and Ahmose supporting their rule by Osirian doctrines rather than through the purely solar cults which had taken over in previous centuries.

Set – it was always Set – became the personification of darkness again; the great arts and styles of the Old Kingdom were recreated; a colossal granite temple for the Apis Bull was built at Saqqara; and the Egyptians were able to imagine for a little while that true greatness had been restored to their land. Ankh-f-n-Khonsu, who lived a full life sometime during those reigns, was the priest who brought about the Aeon of Osiris to replace that of Isis. And, as is the way of magic, he was also the one who brought it to an end.

If Ankh-f-n-Khonsu died in the 26th Dynasty, then at the same time, through one of those tricks understood only by Anubis, he was reborn in 1875, not far from an old tree in Leamington Spa, Warwickshire, which was widely held to be at the exact centre of England. This was also a time historians would come to regard as being the absolute zenith of the British Empire. Later on, his life would continue to echo this local belief in the way that he saw himself as the Omphalos, the divine navel or centre – not merely of England, to which he had an ambivalent attitude, or of the Empire, which was the greatest ever seen – but of the entire world – and perhaps substantial portions of the universe too.

His mother, a prim lady of the narrowest kind, was never to understand all this. There was not much of the compassionate Isis in her. She was never able to see her son as Ankh-f-n-Khonsu, Prince Chioa Khan, Frater Perdurabo, or as any of the many other masks and names he assumed in his extraordinary life. To her, he was simply Edward Alexander Crowley, her difficult son; and if he was to call himself also, more enduringly, Aleister, and claim to be bringing to the world visions from beyond Time, then that was something she did not want to know about at all.

Crowley in fact holds many of the threads that form the warp and woof of this narrative. In due course we will be able to see how these can be pulled together through him to form a garment of pure light. He was, along with his one-time mentor Samuel Liddell 'MacGregor' Mathers, one of those magicians who actively worked at bringing the Egyptian Mysteries out into the consciousness of the West. Mathers was the greater magician, but Crowley had one inestimable advantage: his was one of the most marvellously dreadful, warped, and unforgettable personalities of all time. Yet he used this personality like a crystal boat – a dream-craft able to carry dead (or as yet unawakened) souls with him.

But did he, and many others like him, actually bring the Great Gods of Egypt into the Western consciousness, or were they here already?

Many occultists have argued that the Egyptian mysteries gradually, over vast periods of time, spread westward either via migrating peoples, or traders, taking their gods with them in much the same way that Asian shopkeepers in Britain today have brought Islam, Buddhism, and Hinduism with them. Or else they were brought by conquest, via the Greeks and Romans who had long been heavily influenced by the cults of Isis and Osiris in some form. In her elegant, beautiful and almost incantatory book, *Awakening Osiris*, Normandi Ellis lists some of the words in the modern English language that she feels to be of Egyptian origin:

arm – *armen*
hex – *heku*
nebulous – *neb*
satisfy – *Satis* (goddess of the flood, or meaning 'enough')
aura – *aor* (magic light)[6]

I had forgotten about those words. They make me pause and ponder, and rest my rake along the wall and go Hmmm, which is the nearest I've ever got to the ineffable word of Om.

The lines in my Zen garden are the parallel paths in life we all have. They are the paths that we could label: Could Have Taken/Should Have Taken/Thank God I Didn't Take. There is also the odd and intriguing path that is invariably marked But … What If?

When I was a young man of 22 I spent some time in the University of Kentucky. I didn't go to America to study, I went to find my soulmate and thus the True Love and Happiness I felt sure was over there. Someone who would, for once, be able to share this 'other' side that had always dominated and sometimes bent me out of shape during an era when such things were hardly known.

I took a class on Creative Writing with Wendell Berry. I'd never heard of him and didn't know he already had a fine reputation as a writer, as well as being something of an eco-warrior decades before they coined the term.

One of the girls in the class – the only one I fancied – was lithe and leggy, with exceedingly pretty face, long hair, a quiet presence and lovely voice. I was dreadfully shy in those days but made a clumsy attempt to chat her up. I got nowhere. I don't think she even realised what I was trying to do. I saw her around the campus often, always with

---

6  Normandi Ellis, *Awakening Osiris*. (Grand Rapids, MI: Phanes Press, 1988), p. 23.

a wistful sense of regret. My only consolation was that she would never have understood my 'other' side.

Nearly 40 years later I got an email from a writer that Billie John and I had always looked up to as one of the real ones: Normandi Ellis, who said flattering things about our *Inner Guide to Egypt* which made me glow and blush. It was only when I asked questions about her background that I realised this was She from the Creative Writing class, the one who could not possibly have understood me!

Still, it is said that even if you take the wrong path you always end up at the same place. The still-lovely and gracious Normandi and I, oceans apart, are both in very good places indeed: she on her porch in Kentucky, me on the wall of my Zen garden, and I would not swap my life with that of anyone. Yet I'm still having a little ponder of What If?

If all Western languages can be traced back to an Indo-European original, then we are a step closer to acknowledging that Egyptian influences of more than one sort did indeed spread westward. In a similar vein, J. P. Cohane, who was an etymologist, concluded that 'in ancient times, before the Carthaginians, the Egyptians, the Greeks, and the Romans, certain key names and words were taken out in all directions from the Mediterranean [and have survived] in spite of corruptions, in the names of rivers, mountains, volcanoes and waterfalls, lakes and islands, regions, towns and cities, scattered all across the face of the earth.'[7] He may well be a little over-enthusiastic here, but with such a vast theme it is never any good trying to subtly understate the case. We could, however, take his words and jiggle them about a little:

'In ancient times, certain key names, and words, and religious concepts were taken out in all directions from the Mediterranean. ...' That would be better. It might even be true. And it would also explain why Osirian imagery can be found to underlie some of the more numinous aspects of what has become known as the Western Mystery Tradition.

---

7 J. P. Cohane, *The Key*, quoted by John Ivimy in *The Sphinx and the Megaliths*. (London: 1974)

It has also been argued that the more spectacular examples of megalithic culture in Britain – notably Stonehenge and Avebury – were the creation of Egyptian priest-scientists. Archaeologists and anthropologists were once adamant that similarities between the chambered tombs of Britain and the mastabas built in Egypt in the 3rd millennium B.C. were too close to be altogether accidental. As is usual with such speculation, there are also astronomers, archaeologists, historians and outright magicians who insist the opposite: that the origins of these Mysteries were actually in north-west Europe, and were exported eastward.

Were Aleister Crowley, MacGregor Mathers and all the other magicians in Britain and the West merely responding to a fad in adopting the gods and goddesses of Egypt as their primary inspirations? Or were they really touching upon the exotic origins of their own nation's most ancient mysteries? It would be a simple enough debate if it wasn't for Atlantis.

Many magicians insist, usually on the basis of their own visions, that the true origins of their esoteric heritage can be found even further west, in that sunken land below the Atlantic Ocean. Before Atlantis went down, they insist further, active units of priests and priestesses were sent off in all directions. Some of them made it to Britain and Europe, others to Egypt, either directly by sea, or via various overland routes through Africa. Still others headed westward and thus helped found the Mayan cultures or even – much further north – influenced the North American Indian.

Everything stems from that lost continent, they say. By this, they explain the fundamental similarities between the mythologies and magic of different nations.

If we can resist its seductive appeal for a moment, can we really believe in Atlantis? We can if we want. There will always be enough evidence to support the believers, and never quite enough to sway the sceptics.

The *sense* of Atlantis, however, brings an unmistakable tone: of great age but incomparable vigour; a peculiar sort of pride – such as a Harvard man might feel next to a graduate from a hillbilly institute; and the feeling, indeed the knowledge, that there are sources of real but eldritch power available for you when needed.

The most enduring image from all the Atlantean mythology of

the modern magicians, however, is that of the three-tiered mountain rising from the waters, on top of which lived the priest-kings, the Atlantean elite, the focus of whose lives revolved around the temples dedicated to working with the solar, lunar, and stellar forces. These were the people, it was felt, who influenced the evolution of the world.

We must focus on the mountain, however, rather than the accretions on it. Wipe out the inhabitants, and we are left with Atum's mound above the waters, later echoed by those 'Mounds of Osiris' left behind whenever the water of the Nile had withdrawn. We are left with such bare and pure equivalents as Glastonbury Tor, which is the focus of many Avalonian Mysteries, or with Ayers Rock in Australia, Mt. Kailas, Mt. Shasta – and indeed every emanating power-source which has ever been heaved up beyond the sea level and into human awareness.

We experience Atlantis in our own ways, but we can best deal with it for the moment by regarding it as an Essence, to apply a medieval term. Charles Fielding, the pen-name of the late Alan Adams, a modern magician of formidable experience, asserted that it is not simply a place, but an entire set of conditions that probably went on for at least ten thousand years. 'It was a whole series of civilizations – in both an area and a period of time.'[8]

To describe something as Atlantean is akin to all those American advertisements which evoke the term 'European' to give their product a particular tone, a certain quality. We can believe in an actual place if we need, but for the rest of this book let us accept it as an essence, just as Hollywood is an essence: a place whose true impact and reality is to be found more within the hearts and minds of its admirers than within the concrete of its streets.

Of course, peoples of every nation tend to regard their own lands as being peculiarly sacred, home of the gods, and host to whatever Second Coming is most appropriate. Being an Englishman first and a Briton second, I am no different.

**Do I now, sitting in the calm of my Zen garden believe in the historical existence of Atlantis, whether it was in the mid-Atlantic around the Azores, North Atlantic in the guise of Thule, a distortion of the Minoan**

---

8  Carr Collins and Charles Fielding, *The Story of Dion Fortune*. (New York: Star and Cross Publications, 1985), p. 135

civilisation on Crete, under the Antarctic ice or – as William G. Gray suggested to me – possibly on another planet?

No.

But if I stand at the tip of Brean Down where Dion Fortune based events in her hypnotic novel *The Sea Priestess*, or even – bizarrely – on the rim of the old Marine Lake in nearby Weston-super-Mare, an energy sweeps through me that has incredible age: older than Ancient Egypt or Megalithic Europe, older than the old gods I write about. All reason and logic goes out of my mental window and the sheer power of the flow can only be described as ... Atlantean.

It still doesn't merit a rock in my garden though.[9]

To the peoples of antiquity the isle of Britain was the very home of mystery, a sacred territory, to enter which was to encroach upon a region of enchantment, the dwelling of the gods, the shrine and habitation of a cult of peculiar sanctity and mystical power. Britain was, indeed, the *insula sacra* of the West, an island veiled and esoteric, the Egypt of the Occident.

These are words from *The Mysteries of Britain*, by Lewis Spence, a Scot who had been a member of *An Uileach Druidh Braithreachas* or the Druid Universal Bond[10] and one of those rare types who was able to combine a passion for magic with a genuine scholar's learning, delivered in a wondrously lucid style. Spence may have been writing with no small pride about his native land but his opinions would have been shared completely by Julius Caesar, who came, saw, and finally conquered much of Britain in 55 and 54 B.C. To Caesar's mind, the Druid religion began in that country and found its highest expression there.

Unfortunately the Druids too have become something of an Essence, invariably visualized as cerebral, clean, restrained, and philosophical fellows with white robes and stern miens – rather like

---

9  Incidentally Gray had no interest in Atlantis whatsoever, despite his passion for Dion Fortune.
10 Ithell Colquhoun, *The Sword of Wisdom*. (London: Neville Spearman, 1975). This book contains details about the relationship between the Druid Universal Bond and the Hermetic Order of the Golden Dawn.

castrated versions of the average English Bishop today. But the reality was far different, far more virile, infinitely more savage, and more akin in style to the various shamans of the American continent than anyone else.

This is one of the reasons why reputable pre- and post-War psychics in Britain were bewildered to 'see' what they assumed to be 'Red Indian' or even Mayan communities at the megalithic sites, causing them to speculate on various migratory theories and occult histories. Yet in truth they were seeing native British life in the raw, without the usual Victorian projections.

Britain was known on the continent as the Isle of the Dead, the westernmost world beyond the ocean where young priests were sent to further their training in the Mystery Colleges on Salisbury Plain – an area where Britain now maintains its top-secret aeronautical research establishments, germ warfare laboratories, and a host of military encampments. Even today the Plain, when night is falling, is not a 'nice' place to be.

**That last is true enough. The whole area heaves with witches, dragons, gods and ghosts, phantom Black Dogs, spirit Guardians of ancient sites, hill forts, barrows, colossal earth Zodiacs built into the terrain, crop circles, malign and benign standing stones, echoes of Dark Age and Civil War battles, time slips, earthbound medieval monks, phantom hitch-hikers, faery gates and regular sightings of UFOs. But the real danger these days is that you might wander into the live firing areas used by the British Army and get flattened by a Challenger 2 battle tank with impenetrable Chobham armour.**

Now it was once the fashion to describe magic in terms of 'rays': there was the Egyptian Ray, the Celtic Ray – invariably but misleadingly associated with the Green Ray, a Norse Ray, Christian Ray, and so on. A more useful if cruder analogy, however, can be lifted from the science of geology. Egyptian magic, far from being a ray of light, is more akin to one of those tectonic plates which support whole continents, and which constantly 'drift' across the globe. It is the collision with the tectonic plate of Indian mysticism that has caused tremors, massive surging energies, and disruptions which have raised mountains and nations. It is within these disruptions and break-aways upon the earth's surface that we can find the smaller, but by no means inferior mysteries of the West which found expression among the Germanics and/or Teutons and the rest – all of which overlapped in one way or another.

As we have noted, it is a generally accepted theory about the population of Western Europe that a succession of peoples moved westwards from some point of origin in Asia Minor – the traditional Garden of Eden.

These migrations were like ripples in a pool, each successive ripple of humanity driving the previous incumbents on westward until there was only Britain and Ireland before them. If nothing else, Britain in particular became something of a melting pot, and most of the pantheons of Europe and beyond found expressions there in some form at some time. Millennia later, thanks to individuals and organizations like the Wright Brothers and the Cunard Line, the same thing happened within America, with the same ultimate result.

If there is an Egyptian stratum of consciousness, there is also what might be termed the Avalonian stratum lying somewhere above it. By Avalon is meant a realm which, although linked inseparably to real places, is not entirely within this world. Britain might be the body, but Avalon is the ka, or spirit, in the eyes of many. Egypt had its masculine focus in Osiris, who was the Green Man, Horned King and Horned God: Avalon, in contrast, had King Arthur.

**I was never able to visualise or think in terms of Rays. The idea of 'strata' came to me when out walking in the Midford Valley and I stumbled upon an old cottage which bore a plate saying this had been the home of William Smith, Father of English Geology, who had determined the stratification of the land. As I was in one of my spacey, god-befuddled states at the time I felt that this was meant to tell me something.**

**It certainly did. It enabled me to get the sense of Ancient Egypt as being a stratum of consciousness within me, below or above which might lie other strata that I could dig into for their respective treasures.**

It enabled me to make sense of how, while living on the border of Wiltshire and Somerset, I was able to be obsessed and sometimes possessed by the gods of Khem. Egypt was suddenly no longer a geopolitical location with a troubling Islamic overlay, reachable only after several hours' flight from Britain: it became at once a pure realm at the bottom of my mind.

The 'troubling Islamic overlay' is one of my very many quirks. I cannot associate Egypt today with the culture that I had remote-viewed, or perhaps known in a past life. While I may be sitting on the low wall of my Zen garden in apparent seraphic calm, there are shades of Templars beyond the boundaries and they seem to bristle at the very thought of Islam. I have asked them many times what they want but get no clear reply. In fact I wrote a black-comic novel called *Dark Light* to exorcise them. Still they come.

If the druids have been given the Hollywood treatment (and there is a small joke buried there which would cause any decent Druid to smile) then the same can be said about Arthur – perhaps more so. The image we retain of him is more akin to Richard Coeur de Leon, the Black Prince or the mythical Saint George than anyone else. If Arthur existed at all, then he would have been a dark-haired Celt, someone who fought on foot, and with little of the chivalric manners invested in him by those medieval romancers who came a thousand years after his probable time. He may have historical origins as a Romano-British warlord who held off the Saxons for a brief spell. He may even have been a Breton warlord Arzur who did similar deeds, but his true role for our present purposes is to be found as the Once and Future King – the British Christ in some ways. Like all Sacred Kings, many places within many nations claim him for their own; or, as with Jesus, preserve myths which seek to prove that he once, and right fondly, visited their country.

Arthur is the son of Uther Pendragon. The origin of his name is not clear, although it is invariably linked with artos, 'the bear'. But can we, by listening very carefully to the sheer sound of these names Arthur and Uther, detect a resemblance to the names *As-Ar* and *Us-er*?

The word for 'mother,' for example, has retained its shape and sound ever since its spread from the Indo-European original: Sanskrit – *matr;* Latin – *mater;* Old Irish – *mathir;* Old High German – *muotar;* Old Saxon – *modar;* Old English – *modor;* Old Frisian – *modor;* and Dutch *moeder*.[11]

And here we must distinguish the formal 'mother' from the instinctive labial plosives used by babies when they call for mum, mom, or mummy. This becomes a little more plausible when we note the magical tradition which insists that Arthur was not the name of an individual but an initiatic title. Just as the pharaohs linked with Osiris in their names and titles, so might the name Arthur have been passed down through the kingships as a symbol of role, or function.

Yet before we can go further into this topic, we must pause and take a simplified look at the main details of the Arthurian Cycle. It is not quite as simple a task as dealing with the Egyptian myths, because the latter used pictures – hieroglyphs – to create words and concepts within the mind. The glyphs of the Egyptian pantheons are easy to hang onto, but in the Matter of Britain, as it is called, words are used to evoke pictures.

It is a question of two separate cultures using different sides of the brain. This means we must visualise the Arthurian figures as best we can, seeing them with faces that are already known to us. And before we can do this with any of the better-known figures within the Cycle, we must begin at the beginning. We must look at Uther Pendragon.

Uther is possibly the most darkling of all the characters within the Arthurian Mysteries – although 'character' is perhaps a misleading term when so little is known of his personal qualities. The phonetic similarity between the names of Arthur and Uther is so obvious as to be almost ignored, yet it helps give more substance to the concept of this being an initiatic title. This in itself is given a further boost by the name Pendragon. *Pen* is from the Cornish for 'Head.' So Uther, as Head of the Dragon, or even Dragon King, takes on a special significance when we consider the esoteric concept of the dragon or serpent as a symbol of the Earth's energies, and also as the terrestrial shadow of the Hawk.

---

11 The d letters here are actually variants of the old letter *eth*, ð, pronounced 'th'.

That sounds oh-so clever, almost too clever for me now, even though I agree with him. I think his tone is caused by him being inspired, almost living in two worlds at the same time in those days. But he was also trying a bit too hard to sound like a great Adept and I find that irritating. In fact the last bit about the dragon being the terrestrial shadow of the Hawk is stolen without acknowledgment from the marvellous Kenneth Grant, who really was a great Adept. I'm sitting here peering into my garden at my young self as he wriggles his way through life, and while he was trying to sound wise as a serpent he was probably a bit of a snake at times...

Uther Pendragon fell in love with Ygraine, wife to Gorlois of Cornwall, but the love was not mutual. In fact, his suit was so futile that he was only able to press it further by means of magic. With the aid of Merlin the Enchanter, who enabled him to change shape for one night, he was able to impersonate Gorlois and attain 'the pleasure of Ygraine's thighs', as it was delicately put. As with all such matings, a child was conceived that same night.

This of course was Arthur. Under an arrangement with Ygraine, who soon realized what had happened, Merlin took the child away and fostered him out to the kindly Sir Ector, of the Forest Sauvage, to raise him as his own.

In the interim, Uther made himself High King. He died years later but left no apparent heir. After his death, a miraculous sword was seen plunged irretrievably into an anvil mounted on a stone. This too, it turned out, was a feat which had been engineered by Merlin. The legend on the sword (which was *not* Excalibur) stated that whosoever could pull the sword from the stone would be the rightful King of Britain. Only the boy, Arthur, the Miraculous Child, was able to draw the sword from the anvil – to his own astonishment.

It was then that Sir Ector revealed Arthur's true origins. Gradually the lesser kings accepted him. In due course, Merlin appeared once more to lead him toward a mystic lake wherein the arm of a Lady 'clothed in white samite' rose from the depths of the lake bearing the sword Excalibur and its marvellous scabbard.

We might pause at this natural juncture and look at this a little more closely:

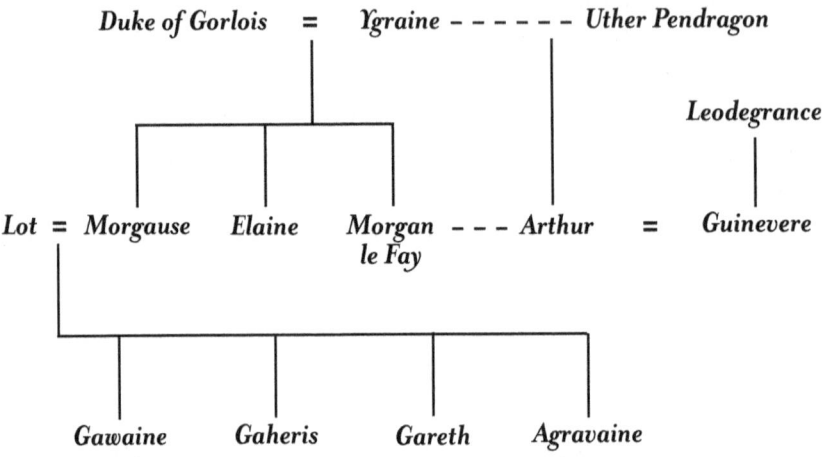

**Arthur's Family Tree**

It was the magician Violet Firth, writing under the pen-name Dion Fortune, who hinted that the story of Ygraine, Uther, and Gorlois was in fact a shadowy version of cross-fertilization between a royal woman of Atlantean stock and one of the native Britons. The child would necessarily be 'of the Blood,' as she thought of it – a prince of the Sacred Clan which had once ruled Atlantis. This concept of the Blood Royal, or the Sang-Real, has persisted in various lines of mystical theory and magical practice down through to the present day. Dion Fortune was inclined to believe that she had been an Atlantean priestess herself in a previous life. She had certainly spent many other lives working in temples along the Nile.[12]

That is one of the interpretations. Another, not necessarily contradictory approach might be that Uther was not so much a physical person but in fact a Kingly spirit on the inner planes, and one who overshadowed Gorlois so completely that one of the love-makings with his wife became transformed into something more than that, opening Gates between the worlds and the womb which would allow a Son or Daughter of Light to incarnate.

---

12 Alan Richardson, *Priestess, the Life and Magic of Dion Fortune.* (Wellingborough, UK: Aquarian Press, 1986).

This happens. It can happen to one or both partners when it is necessary for a soul of a particular type and destiny to be born. Sons and Daughters of Light do not always function in philosophical or religious areas of life. They are not always apparent to the masses. Sometimes they can seem to be dangerous characters indeed. And sometimes, when they just fail to express their Light in the proper manner, they really can become dangerous, even if they are sparked with something sublime. The fact that Merlin was involved points to the idea that this was not merely an act of magically arranged rape, but the sort of ritually charged sexual magic that was well-known and perhaps fundamental to Mystery Centres throughout the Classical world.

Whichever interpretation we choose, we are still left with the concept of a sexual act linked with magical practices that result in a child touched with divinity.

**I have found over many decades that many magicians and mystics go through a phase wherein they feel themselves involved in work of global and also cosmic importance. They feel that the world will suffer if it is not recognised/published/trumpeted immediately. When they first get plugged in to what might be called a Magical Current they have a tremendous sense of immanence – of something or Someone coming. They feel themselves to be Hermetic versions of John the Baptist, lone voices calling out in the wilderness, waiting for the Messiah to appear. If they have no-one to guide them, or if they are unlucky, they then begin to think:** *Hang on, maybe it is me who is immanent, maybe I am the Chosen One.*

**The feeling of immanence, I would suggest, having experienced it myself, is to do with making clear links to your own Higher Self. The individual can get confused by interpreting this experience, this blossoming light and consciousness, in terms of Judaeo-Christian imagery.**

**One man I knew, a magician of raw but very real power, suddenly started to get visions of himself winning the Superbowl in the US, and thousands chanting his name. 'It will happen Alan. It will happen,' he assured me, while trying to get me to become a sort of Baptist figure myself, and give him due recognition. I couldn't.**

That was over 30 years ago. I think he's living in a caravan near Southend now.

He was a nice man though, and I learned a lot from him.

---

But despite the specious similarities which can be drawn between Uther/Us-er and Arthur/As-Ar, we are not yet firmly within the realms of Osirian parallels.

These begin to manifest more clearly in Arthur's adult life, as will be shown. So far, all we need is to acknowledge that Arthur and Osiris were both kings – and indeed both Divine Kings; that they were linked with the concept of illuminated rulership; and that their names became used as initiatic titles for those who followed.

Can we, however, find any clear Osirian parallels which link that god with the image of the dragon, or winged serpent, and thus show that the name Pendragon, too, really may have been more than just a family name? Yes, we can. In The Book of Caverns we can see a very clear image of Osiris, deep in the Earth, enfolded by a serpent. This is Wer, 'Most Ancient One', or Nehaher, 'Fearful Face', or Mehen, 'Encircler'. To Egyptians, all the serpents or dragons were one, all linked with the Underworld, and both protective and retarding as all Earth energies can be. For Osiris to 'rise up,' the serpent had to be controlled, the telluric energies harnessed.

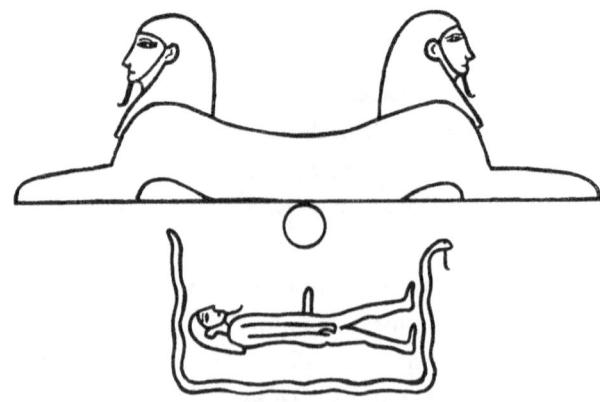

*Osiris in the Underworld enfolded by the serpent and guarded by Aker*

In light of this, we can regard Arthur as one who 'pens' or controls the dragon, thereby taking Pendragon in its English rather than Cornish interpretation. And, of course, the uraeus, the serpent symbol on the brow, came to be considered a supreme emblem of all the pharaohs' power.

But what of Merlin? Although magicians, drawing on their qabalahs, have invariably associated him with the Ibis-headed figure of Thoth, he will soon show himself to be far more akin to Anubis. In an age when it is customary to analyse every goddess figure as something of a Triple Goddess (Maiden/Mother/Crone), we often forget that gods, too, can split themselves.

Hermes, Thoth, and Anubis can in fact be seen as differing aspects of the one entity, being at once revealer and scribe of that which is revealed, at once Chthonian and Olympian, at once Gold and Black, above and below ... this is the god who travels between the realms of humanity and divinity, linking one to the other. Merlin himself does exactly this, and contains within himself both the Horned God and the Black Dog.

In fact the Arthurian Cycle would surely fall apart without Merlin. He weaves himself in and out of it; he appears at crucial moments and indeed instigates these moments. In this respect he is like time itself, and also fate, for he brings into being certain incidents which hurry the cycle along to its terrible end. He is also, in his Anubic role as a symbol of breeding, clearly shown as responsible for the continuation of the Pendragon bloodline.

There is no doubt that Merlin is more than a mere magician: he is the High Priest; he is the tester and confirmer of Kings – and Divine Kings at that. It was he who created the sword in the stone through which Arthur proved who and what he was.

Now, to the mind of the Ancient Britons, the sword was, *par excellence*, the weapon of choice for the royal and rich. A prestige weapon. Anyone could make a spear, but a sword could only be made through the most sophisticated technologies of the time, making use of the raw materials to be found within the Earth.

Arthur's pulling the sword out of the anvil, which itself was placed upon a great stone, is a symbol of man controlling the ores and Elements of the Earth, and using his intelligence to shape and (eventually) wield them. This is true Dragon mastery – an idea made more pertinent by the dragon/serpent/phallic imagery inherent within the sword. Pulling the sword from the stone proved Arthur's kingship on outer levels to the massed lesser kings, but it was not confirmed on inner levels until he had been given Excalibur.

Again, it is Merlin who leads him to the appropriate lake in which Vivienne the Enchantress lives. The sword and its scabbard is given to the King by the Lady, who is seen as no more than an arm rising above the misty waters. In this tale, the sheer importance of the scabbard over that of the sword itself is emphasized. The sword can destroy, but the scabbard heals. The sexual symbolism is obvious here again. The sword within the scabbard = the penis in the vagina = Man and Woman (and humanity) in perfect union.

Excalibur can therefore be seen as an image of the Dragon rising into the King's hand from the primeval depths. It can also be seen in a purely phallic sense, as the lost sexual organ of Osiris given back to the King to make him complete. It had been swallowed by a fish, remember, a singular aspect of the Piscean symbol for the present Age. It is given to him by the Lady of the Lake. However we choose to concentrate on specific images, the basis of the tale is that it is through Woman that Man can find himself, and all the healings that he might need.

Once this completion of the spirit is attained, he becomes 'the divine man-child, the heir of eternity, self-begotten and self-born, King of Earth and Prince of the Underworld.' These words apply exactly to the young Arthur at the moment when he accepts Excalibur, but they were written about Ra-Hera-khty, or Ra-Hoor-Khuit, as Ankh-f-n-Khonsu would have called him.

Had Arthur been an Egyptian, he would have been granted the right to wear the crowns of the Upper and Lower Kingdoms at that moment, wield the crook and flail, wear the uraeus on his brow and become the exact balance to his predecessor, Osiris, in the Underworld just as Horus was in the outer world. As one descends into the Earth, the other soars into the sky. They balance each other in endless orbit.

Now comparative mythology is a dangerous topic for the dogmatist and pedant – especially those with what might be termed a qabalistic cast of mind. It is almost impossible, for example, to make one-to-one comparisons. There are extraordinary similarities between the Egyptian and Avalonian systems, but they are not exactly the same.

The Mysteries of Egypt, for example, vibrate at a far slower frequency than those of Avalon.

The Mysteries of Egypt established themselves and were fully recorded in various ways over thousands and thousands of years, while the Mysteries of Avalon were fragmented, distorted, and almost destroyed. So there will always be differences. Nevertheless, we can use the hard details of these two mythologies like pieces of flint: if we bring them together sharply enough, and at an appropriate angle, they will make sparks, they will bring Light.

What we can see, so far, are themes of the Magical Mating, the Wondrous Child, and the idea of kingship that is ratified on divine levels but is yet intrinsically connected with the land.

Arthur, it should be seen, was a Triple figure in his own right as Child, Priest-King, and eventually Sacrificed God. It is at the juncture between leaving his Childhood and becoming a Priest-King that he receives Excalibur. It is from then on that he becomes, like Osiris in his 'Green Man' aspect, inextricably linked and identified with the fertilities and fortunes of the kingdom he rules.

Arthur becomes High King then, and establishes himself at Camelot – the precise location of which is claimed exclusively by the Welsh, Scots, Bretons and English as being within their borders alone. Just as they all claim Arthur himself for their own, they also argue with scholarly brilliance and little agreement that the whole Cycle was an expression of the Mysteries of their own particular nation. They support their arguments at all points with references to ancient texts, local place names, and legends.

People outside the British Isles rarely appreciate the intensity with which the Welsh and Scots feel themselves to be nations apart, and only connected with that conglomerate known as Great Britain by circumstances of unhappy histories. Even within England, certain regions insist upon Arthurian locations of their own. The only truth can be that Camelot is a movable city. It is that area within our consciousness which is able to contain the figures of its myth. Camelot is an inner temple of vast size and splendour which we must all find within ourselves. Like Atlantis, like Arthur, Camelot is an essence. Take all the glamour from all the castles of Britain and Europe, all the glory from all the tales of chivalrous combat, then wrap them around some bleak and windswept hill-fort like the swathes around a mummy, and you have a place and a name which almost sings. Camelot is mankind looking back with nostalgia towards its infancy. Our childhood homes seem tinged with wonder, mysterious and scarcely comprehensible places which are always vast in the memory but unbelievably small and invariably decrepit when we visit them in reality as adults.

But however humble the kingdom and its capital, a King must necessarily have a Queen. A suitable wife was accordingly found by the name of Guinevere, and brought with her, as her father's wedding gift, the Round Table. The best knights in the world were to sit around this. No man could sit at its head, and all were equal with the King. In other words, they were a living parallel to the Zodiac – intensely individual souls who were, nevertheless, interacting parts of a corporate whole. Merlin – again – inscribed each place with the name of the knight who would occupy it.

Their names today provoke echoes of romance and pageantry that are unequalled in the West: Galahad, Perceval and Bors; Gareth, Gawaine and Gaheris ... The list becomes too large for such a finite object as the Table had to be. But then, it never existed on this plane at all. Of them all, it was Galahad who would achieve the greatest destiny on spiritual levels when he became one of the two knights to attain the Holy Grail. Even so, for a long time, the popular imagination held that his father was really the best knight. This was Lancelot of the Lake, who was soon to bring Camelot crashing down for no other reason than that he loved too well ...

The name Guinevere comes from Gwynhwyfar, which has been interpreted as 'White Shadow' or 'White Phantom.' This has obvious echoes with the figure of Gwyn ap Nudd whom we will look at in the next chapter, whose name means 'Light Son of Darkness' – put the comma where you will. Gwynhwyfar could equally be translated as 'Light from the Shadow.'

In this, can we find some hint of an initiatic name given to the wife of the Horned God? We can if we want. It might be a deliberate mistranslation, but it bears magic.

She is in many ways the pivot of the Cycle – that aspect which turns it toward tragedy rather than triumph. In some ways she is Maat, bringing order and pattern into the court (via the Round Table). In other ways, she is the representative of the Earth in Spring.

... the fecundity maiden who has to be fertilized that the earth shall bring forth joy and abundance. This is the story of the Mother Earth, first as a fair maiden, the May Queen in white or pale green, crowned with flowers, the magical virgin with whom the God or hero mates to bring back the Earth to fertility ... Then the maiden becomes the bountiful matron of the fruits of the Earth in harvest time.[13]

But, to the dismay of all, Guinevere proved completely infertile when it came to the crucial matter of providing the country with another Pendragon to perpetuate the Cycle. However, she did something which was to affect the whole of her world and worlds to come. What she did was quite extraordinary. There would be nothing like it in Europe with quite the same impact – not until the English yeomen mastered the use of the longbow to slaughter the entire nobilities of France, or Patton's army swept across the Carentan Peninsula and flamed its way toward Berlin, or until a large and strange cloud was seen above Alamogordo in 1944, at the ending and beginning of an Age. What Guinevere did was quite simple: she fell in love. In some ways, she took us all with her.

I sit on a brightly-coloured deckchair aside my garden with my feet on the wall. It is a fine, warm day during a sublime English Spring. When I am not raking and reviewing my patterns, I like to read. Before I went into my non-intellectual phase I would devour every book on Magic that came into my orbit, with a vast and retentive memory for all the details therein. It was Eliphas Lévi who said that if he were ever cast away on a desert island, then he would get all the knowledge he needed from studying the tarot. I wouldn't go that far, during these musing years of mine, but I sometimes think on what 22 books I would take onto my own desert island in place of the tarot trumps.

Dion Fortune's novels *The Sea Priestess* and *Moon Magic* would be first. Marion Campbell's sublime *Dark Twin* would be third. And fourth would be Wendy Berg's *Red Tree, White Tree* which is one of the very few tomes in the past three decades to give me goose pimples of delight and wonder.

---

13 Veronica Ions, *Egyptian Mythology*. (London: Newnes Books, 1965), p. 112.

It details her inner contact with Gwenevere as a Faery Queen, a powerful otherworld being whose interest in linking with us exasperating Humans is evolutionary, benign, and really is crucial to us all.

As I read about my early attempts to make sense of the great myths and legends of the Western Mystery Tradition, I see that the story-tale figures behind them were always real. They used the imagery of Malory, Chrétien de Troyes, T.H. White, Tolkien and countless others to reach into my head and heart and give a silent but hugely potent Hello.

They are doing that to you now, as you read. When you become aware of them, they become aware of you. It is nothing to do with me.

It is generally held these days that the idealization of love, and the concept of Romantic Love, were not something that had existed since the beginning of Time, but were in fact brought into something of a flowering only as recently as the 11th and 13th centuries through the influence of the Troubadours, Minnesingers, and all those writers and storytellers who developed the concept. Prior to that, whatever considerable feelings a man might hold for his woman was always completely subsidiary to his loyalty for and duty toward his lord. Nothing would or should come before that.

So what happened between Lancelot and Guinevere was almost unbelievable, staggering. It does not matter that they may never have existed as historical personages. Their images are real enough within the dream-world of the psyche at least. The story of that romance helped awaken within women – and not a few men – the possibility that there could be more to a husband and wife relationship than mere childbearing.

No, Guinevere had no earthly child, but on other levels she gave birth to Love instead.

That sounds mawkish now but I still think it is true. Yet it was never a cutesy-poo, huggy-feely, smashey-and-nicey birth: it was a bomb going off, with shrapnel zinging everywhere down the ages.

When I met my own earthly analogue of Guinevere she and her husband were American exchange-students at my college. She was golden, gorgeous and well out of my league, I thought, as I watched her trialling (unsuccessfully) for the college band Earthrise, run by young Gordon Sumner. I so envied her husband and wondered what she saw in him, apart from his wealth.

Yeats said about his soul mate Maude Gonne that when he met her he knew that the troubling of his life was about to begin, and I knew exactly what he meant when this analogue of Guinevere turned her awesome attention onto me. Why me, I wondered? and had to put it down to impulses that must have been to do with past lives, and possibly 7th Century Lindisfarne, because it certainly wasn't to do with my puny college grant or the cool, two-tone flares I wore called Loons.

Later, in the States, one of the reasons I never really pressed my suit of the lovely young Normandi Ellis was that I was already being tipped by this new enchantress (I will call her Gee) into the Eternal and Infernal Triangle which echoed that of Arthur, Guinevere and Lancelot.

It brought me the *hieros gamos*, guilt, despair, far memories, holy beauty, and a very real descent toward breakdown. Looking back at my turbulent emotional life before and since I see that I have been in Arthur's place many times; I have even been in Guinevere's role, in loving two others equally; but I know Lancelot the best because of Gee, though I've only been in his angle once. When Lancelot's mind broke for the love of his Queen and he had to spend time as a Wild Man in a forest, I was there in the trees with him; burned-out wrecks, both of us.

Yet in a sense it gave me the very deep happiness I have today, and has enabled me to build at least one of the walls of this garden with the bricks of experience it provided.

Given the magic, the numinosity, the poetry, the moments of sublimity and the life-changing nature of being in that triangle which helped make me what I am now, would I go through it again?

No.

In the romance *Perceval le Gallois*, Guinevere is in fact shown in greater depth than the popular tales allow:

> ... there has never been a lady of such renown for, just as the wise master teaches young children, my lady the queen teaches and instructs every living being. From her flows all the good in the world, she is its source and origin. Nobody can take leave of her and go away disheartened for she knows what each person wants and the way to please each according to his desires. Nobody observes the way of Rectitude or wins honour unless they have done so from my lady, or can suffer such distress that he leaves her still possessed of his grief.

If Arthur is to be associated with Osiris, can we see echoes of Isis within Guinevere? Only so much as we can see Isis in all Women. In other respects, the answer has to be no. After all, Isis' love was for her brother, keeping it in the family as did many noble families throughout the world. Isis is perhaps not the best one to follow or invoke when you first fall in love: She comes to cope with the problems that inevitably follow after this initial state. Guinevere, in contrast, comes to us from the start. She is even there before the start of any love match. She has not yet come into her own.

**When I wrote that last short sentence I was using literary style and technique to imply that I knew more than I dare say to the uninitiated, or the mere neophyte. Which is a joke, really, in that I've never had and never will accept any kind of initiation into anything, so I'm the biggest Beginner you'll ever meet. But there is a way in which it *is* true. Thanks to Wendy's book, and a completely unexpected appearance from an entity I can only call du Lac, perhaps Guinevere has now come into her own. At least within my psyche.**

So Guinevere fell in love with Lancelot, and he loved her in return to the point of madness, almost torn apart by this and his duty toward his beloved King. It was this love which brought the whole Camelot and the Realm tumbling down. Like Osiris, the Holy Realm of Logres was to be torn part, and bits of the magical edifices scattered over the known world.

In many ways the importance of the Arthurian Cycle is to be found in the matings and the marriages – and in the children that were or were not born as a result.

There was: Elaine, daughter of that Fisher-King who ruled the wasteland and guarded the Holy Grail. She pretended to be Guinevere one dark night and tricked Lancelot into sleeping with her – much as Nephthys slept with Osiris. The result of the union was Galahad, the pure and perfect youth who was to find that Holy Grail. And Morgan le Fay, the great Witch-Queen who used magic in order to sleep with her half-brother, Arthur, in an echo both of Nephthys again and of the brother-sister matings among the pharaohs. Both Elaine and Morgan were 'magical' women with peculiar Otherworld associations.

It is almost as though the unforeseen sterility of Guinevere forced the priesthood that worked behind the scenes to find other ways of perpetuating the Pendragon Mysteries – not for their own purposes, but to ensure the continuation of the land's fertility and life on all levels. It all devolved upon the concept:

The land and its people are one; the King and the Land are One.

As it was, through the resulting children of Galahad and Mordred, the whole Cycle was taken into some completely unexpected directions.

The Round Table was, and is, a symbol of universal order. Camelot was almost like a cross section of some great world axis; it was the centre of the nation, radiating its energies outward. In the light of those two axioms quoted above, an ordered, balanced, and harmonious court would mean the same thing in village, town, district, and kingdom.

The actual image of a Round Table does not appear in Ancient Egypt – unless you count the circular passage of the sun across the Earth and through the Underworld – but the concept behind it does. In fact, the Whole land was a manifestation of the concept:

> ... the sacred geography of ancient Egypt corresponded precisely with the realms of the dead, so that the 42 provinces of the Upper and Lower Kingdoms mirrored the 42 provinces of the Judges of the Dead, the Upper Gods of the Orbit, and the Lower Gods of the Horizon. And all of these were mirrored in the Great Pyramid, the "House of the Hidden Places," so that when the initiate completed his journey through the

labyrinths of the Pyramid of Light, and had emerged above, illumined, he had therefore simultaneously mastered and transcended all the worlds, which were mirrored within the Pyramid itself.¹⁴

As above, so below; as without, so within.

Intriguingly, we can catch glimpses of this in Britain too in circular Earth-zodiacs that more and more researchers are finding in the topography of various regions. These zodiacs are formed by the natural features of the land, and are only perceivable from the air or on detailed maps, and are invariably linked with local mystery centres of vast age and sanctity. The most famous of these is at Glastonbury in Somerset, which is a town with more Arthurian associations than most.

**I don't care if Dion Fortune described it as the Holyest Earthe in England, I can't stand the place. When I was a teenager, long before the enormous festivals, when all the cafés had signs on the doors saying 'No Hippies', Glastonbury attracted only the cognoscenti, who whispered its name from mouth to ear, archly, as if it was the Lost Word of the Masons.**

**The first time I climbed the Tor I had a vision of giant figures surrounding it (though I had not heard of the supposed Zodiac then) and came down with a splitting headache. Have been up many times since but have never soared. Now the place has become to the New Agers (if I might still use that term) what the Vatican is to the Catholic Church, and seems to be creating the kind of Alternative Orthodoxy which is the death-knell for true Mysteries. Hordes of pilgrims today make their way lemming-like up the spiral path to the Tor's summit and throw themselves off into an increasingly Disneyfied version of Avalon.**

**Those of you who have diplomas describing yourselves as trained and initiated Priests and Priestesses of Avalon should fold them into paper boats and sail them off down the River Naradek.**

**My personal spleen apart (which must always be ignored or challenged but never indulged) I would insist that you can – must – find your own sacred hills, groves and earth zodiacs and not limit yourself.**

---

14 Arthur Versluis, *The Egyptian Mysteries* (London: Arkana, 1988), p.76.

Guinevere, then, helped bring this sense of order and pattern to the court both via the stability that any Queen should bring to a kingdom and also through the Round Table that was brought along with her. This is the significance of the throne symbol which appears in the tarot card known as The Empress.

Guinevere, as the constructive force within Nature and society, encouraged the tradition-oriented cohesion of the collective. Through her establishment in the court, conditions were created in which the institutions of law and order could take root. After that, a pattern of learning and spiritual ethics were laid down which would allow the quality of mercy to modify and shape the otherwise ferocious militarism of the Table's members. Guinevere, in brief, was the power of womanhood in the process of creating civilization.

For a time it all went wondrously well. Arthur was a just and strong ruler; the court became the centre of miracles. Magical harts, Green Knights, and ladies in distress appeared, which lured individual knights off on quests that would test their prowess and their goodness and add to the splendour of Camelot. It was only after some time that Arthur suspected what the rest of the court had long known – that the Queen was in love with his champion; that Guinevere was in love with Lancelot. Forces were unleashed that tore society apart – forces every bit as luminous and devastating as those which arise in splitting the atom.

Today, we might learn to use those forces in a process of fusion rather than fission. We can learn to reconstruct ourselves with them – and our futures also.

**Sounds good, but I'm buggered if I know exactly what the lad meant by that last.**

The key to much of the magic discussed or alluded to in the present book is to be found in the figure of Lancelot of the Lake, son of Ban of Benoic. Benoic is a place most usually regarded as being in France but which is often claimed by the Scots as theirs. Thomas Malory, in contrast, gives the seat of Lancelot's power as Bamburgh Castle in Northumberland. This was the original Castle Dolorous which Lancelot himself renamed 'Joyous Gard', after falling in love. Clearly, he was a man with high hopes for this new love affair.

The second rock in my Zen garden represents the volcanic outcrop on which the present day Bamburgh Castle is perched. I place it slightly off-centre, so that most of the raked patterns swirl around its base at some point. I also create a little miniature lake, shaped like a foetus, curled around one part of it, reflecting the mass in its clear waters. In that upside-down reflection, Faery can be found.

There is a powerful myth of transformation connected with Bamburgh Castle which involves a dragon known as the Laidly Worm, a hero known as Childe Wind, witchcraft, treacherous love, powerful women and spell craft. Track them down yourselves if they call to you. Those things never drew me as a boy living not far from there, but the thought of Lancelot changing its name from Castle Dolorous to Joyous Gard made me tingle. I saw him not as this grizzled, remote and scary warrior, but as a hopeful young man with a dazzling face, glowing with wonder at having pulled Guinevere.

This is the old, old wisdom: Be very careful what you invoke for in magic, because you might be unlucky – and get it.

Lancelot was without doubt the most formidable fighting man of his time – or of any time. No one could defeat him in combat by fair means or foul. Strong beyond compare, gallant to an hypnotic degree, brave to the point of madness, and also humble, gentle, and utterly devoted to the King. He was, they all knew, 'the best knight in the world.' He is what all men would imagine themselves to be at heart, in essence, in some way. Like Horus, his time is not yet arrived – not quite.

Like Horus, he is raised and taught to fight by Women of Magic; in this case, by the Lady of the Lake – the same one who had given Arthur the sword Excalibur – who must be seen as something akin to the Queen of Faery. The mystic ladies who grouped themselves around this Queen taught the strange young boy all that he needed to know about the arts of war in a clear parallel to Horus' upbringing in the marshes of the Delta where Isis and Nephthys brought him up to challenge and defeat Set. In both cases, there are dim memories evoked of an obscure Celtic tradition that it was once women, not men, who first taught boys the skills of war.

If the romance between Lancelot and Guinevere can be regarded as something of a prophetic dream – for the race, rather than the individual – then it is the Troubadours whom we must thank for giving voice and words to such dreams. Men and women, they were more than mere singers wandering from castle to castle; they were vibrant expressions of an attitude and emotion completely new to the times in which they lived. In the courts of what we now know as France, they created an atmosphere of culture and amenity toward womankind which nothing had hitherto approached. Their songs were heavily perfumed with those Gnostic or Dualist philosophies the Roman Church would soon do its best to destroy. So they created this mode of "courtly love" that gradually altered the whole shape of Western civilization. Whether they simply expressed a current that was welling up within the psyche or whether their movement initiated that current is a matter for debate.

Certainly Jehane de Notredame was sufficiently impressed by them to write a history in the year 1575, some 400 years or more later, entitled *Les vies des plus célèbres et anciens poètes provençaux*. He also attempted some history moulding himself when he wrote his famous prophecies under the name Nostradamus.

It was a man from this tradition, Chrétien de Troyes, whom we have to consider in any analysis of the Arthurian Cycle. After all, Lancelot did not appear until 1170 when Chrétien mentioned him in the list of Arthur's knights in his work *Erec*. It is he who first mentions that knight's love for Guinevere, and we first hear of the Holy Grail from him. Apparently working under the patronage of Eleanor of Aquitaine, it is Chrétien who was largely responsible for recording some images that we are still following today, like markings on a dusty road.

But there is a curious aspect to the literary figure of Lancelot. If we are to grab him by the shoulders and turn him around, we find that, like Janus, he faces two ways. The face to the rear is indeed that of another knight entirely. It is the face of Gawaine.

The name Gawaine is derived either from Gwalchmai or Gwalchwyn, meaning the Hawk of May or the White Hawk, respectively. Robert Graves regarded them as decidedly mystical names, while Jessie Weston advanced the theory that Gawaine was the first Grail winner. Perhaps in this context the White Hawk is a decidedly coy translation: let us make him into the Hawk of Light instead. It is almost as if Gawaine is Lancelot's alter-ego.

Chrétien, for example, often uses Gawaine to make contrasts with du Lac, as Lancelot is often called. In the unfinished *Le Conte du Graal* (unfinished because Chrétien was burned to death in mysterious circumstances), the two knights undertake parallel adventures. The difference is that Gawaine does not seek the Grail itself but for the bleeding Lance which drips into it. Some authorities tend to dismiss Lancelot entirely as no more than an extended version of Gawaine, and point out that in some sources it is the latter who becomes Guinevere's lover, not du Lac. But there is more to it than that.

What seems to have happened is that Gawaine, a fine knight, became regarded as a symbol of what could be achieved by martial prowess and physical strength. Lancelot, however, became an expanded symbol to show what he could and should have achieved, not through strength alone but through power and love conjoined. Gawaine fails in the *Queste del Saint Graal* because he relies exclusively on prowess, refuses to seek the help of divine grace, and remains blind to the spiritual significance of the Grail. It is Lancelot who has come to progress further spiritually; it is Lancelot who most inspires our affections. Perhaps it is most accurate to say that du Lac was created as Gawaine's higher self, and it was Lancelot who was the symbol through which we could invoke a peculiar quality of love in the ages to come.

So let us go a step further and say that the avatar of the Aeon of Horus, as Ankh-f-n-Khonsu called this Age more commonly known as the Age of Aquarius (the Water-carrier), will be Gawaine/Lancelot: the Hawk of May and the great du Lac.

I find this startling. I do not remember writing this at all. I suppose my initial aim was to make my older self appear wise and witty by having a dig at my callow youth and get a cheap laugh, but this stops me in my tracks and makes me go quiet. Little wonder that my young self was unable to concentrate on packing the groceries in Asda that time.

The lad was on fire.

I agree with all he said.

There are indications of this in the so-called Gnostic Gospels:

> But when the nature of mankind has been taken up and a generation of men moved by my voice comes close to me, thou (John) who hearest me now, wilt have become the same and that which is will no longer be.

This, from the apocryphal Acts of John, alludes to the tradition that at the end of our Age it will be John, the beloved disciple, who will be raised to become the next light-bringer.

Of course, the John-equivalent in the Arthurian Cycle is clearly Lancelot – for which knight was more beloved of Arthur than Lancelot? The very essence of the tragedy is that this great knight loved his King beyond all men – but his Queen beyond life itself.

The moral dilemma tore him apart and drove him to madness and set him off along the path of what Joseph Campbell describes as Separation, Initiation and Return. He became a forest-dweller, a wild man confronting demons in the wilderness of his psyche. If Arthur, in one of the Welsh poems, made a descent into the Underworld to win a cauldron – a sort of proto-Grail – then Lancelot did much the same through his love for Guinevere.

Lancelot was, and is, the wish-fulfilment of the Western spirit, an incarnation of Love and Power. He is the god-form of the New Age – a telesmic image born out of the ruins of Mordred (of whom more presently) based upon Gawaine, and deliberately created to enable consciousness to function on certain lines. Lancelot never existed in the historical sense, but everyone contains his foetus within his or her subconscious, locked away behind that symbol for the Underworld floating and dreaming within the amniotic fluid of his or her dreams.[15]

It was a mysterious mating between du Lac and Elaine (daughter of the Osiris-like Fisher King) which produced Galahad, one of the two Grail winners, whose chastity and purity enabled them to leave this realm entirely and spend infinities within some Christian heaven. Lancelot, in contrast, although granted a vision of the Grail Ceremony, was denied the full attainment because of his sins with Guinevere.

Sins? As an old and dying man, his final confession began: "I have loved a Queen beyond compare, and I have loved her an exceedingly long time ..."

Confession? It is a hymn to love.

**In the summer of 2013, while on a walking holiday on the Isle of Wight, du Lac came through to me with real power. I wrote a novella about him called simply *du Lac*, letting him speak for himself, but filtered through all my own quirks and peccadillos. As I said in the Warning that I used instead of a Preface:**

He first came into my head when I was about 7. I was no infant prodigy so I must have been reading a simple book about the Knights of the Round Table. It was not the jousting, derring-do and sword-play which struck me but the few paragraphs about the chaste Galahad and Perceval attaining the Holy Grail while Lancelot of the Lake had to stand outside and watch.

I had an intuitive understanding of this Holy Grail thing but the word 'chaste' was a new one. I asked my Mam what it meant but she gave me a funny look and made me go and wash behind my ears.

Although I could thrum to the splendour of the Grail experience this was overshadowed by the indefinable sense of injustice that I felt with regard to du Lac. It left me with a kind of controlled sadness, always pulling back from a certain despair. It never quite went away.

He burst into my consciousness again some 30 years later with some power – perhaps because I knew only too well what the word 'chaste' meant

---

15 There are strong links here with Harsaphes (or Herishef), a local God of Heracleopolis Magna in the Faiyum. Harsaphes was a ram-deity represented by a ram-headed man. He was a God of Fertility connected with water, and his name means "He who is on the Lake." As a national deity he was considered to be a specialized form of Horus.

by then. I felt compelled to write an essay 'The Depths of the Lake' which attempted to put across his viewpoint. It has been reprinted in various journals many times since.

Although I have modified/evolved/changed my opinions completely about many things in the esoteric field over several decades, I am still certain about this: if du Lac was denied heaven because he wasn't chaste, because he had loved too much and unwisely and done stupid things for love, then the Holy Grail itself and the Heaven it offered was not worth a spit.

I don't know whether du Lac is a wild ancestral faery being, a magical current using a human image to express itself, an historical member of the del Acqs family, or an archetype resonating to various tetchy aspects of my own personality. Or perhaps bits and pieces of all these. But when he came galloping into my psyche again in the summer of 2013 ... I had no choice but to agree to tell his story.

I had forgotten all about his appearance in the first edition of *Earth God Rising*. No wonder he was pissed off with me. I must now make sure the rock representing him and Bamburgh is fixed very firmly on the ground of my Zen garden.

Now I can't wait to read on...

Who could care about two virginal little prigs like Galahad and Perceval when there is a figure like du Lac to aspire toward? Lancelot turns his back on the sterile heaven of the Christian Grail and becomes a Western bodhisattva, in essence.

To appreciate him a bit more, however, we must look more closely at his alter-ego of Gawaine, as a version of Horus. According to the magician Kenneth Grant, who has long worked directly with the Magical Currents initiated by Ankh-f-n-Khonsu:

> The Horus-hawk ... represents the power of transcending earth. Its terrestrial shadow is symbolised by the dragon ... the beast that devours the solar god...[16]

---

16 Kenneth Grant, *Aleister Crowley and the Hidden God*. (London: Muller, 1973).

Hmmm... so I did acknowledge Aossic after all. I wrote to Kenneth Grant on numerous occasions, and always regret that I never got around to meeting him. I did ask him once if I could 'do' him in terms of biography. As I was walking down Milsom Street in Bath, on the morning he must have read my letter, I had the strangest feeling that he came inside my head to look me over. By return of post he declined my offer graciously. Which is just as well because I would not really have understood or appreciated the strange Currents that flowed through him.

Nor, I often suspect, would Crowley himself.

We know already that Gawaine is the Hawk of May, or the Hawk of Light; we read that his strength waxes before noon, wanes after it; we know about his connection with the Pendragon, who is in fact his uncle; and we can see his connection with Lancelot when we find that the only traceable meaning for that name is from a Germanic root meaning "land."

Further, Gawaine bore the device of the pentagram upon his shield, while this same symbol is a positive attribution of Horus. The words Horus and Aries may reflect one another. Additionally, we learn that Aries in the zodiac also represents that Green Man, the 'Vernal Power of the Sun', which links us with the story of the Green Knight that is so vital to Gawaine. Again, there is the tradition that power is passed down through the sister's son, on the principle that the purity of the blood-line is thus certain – and Gawaine is nephew to the King on his mother's side.

It is via his mystical adventure with the Green Knight, however, that we glide almost effortlessly back into the realms of pure Osirian symbolism. The basic story is described in a superbly evocative, alliterative epic poem of unknown authorship entitled Sir Gawain and the Green Knight. It goes as follows:

On New Year's Day, a gigantic knight appears in Arthur's court, clad entirely in green, riding a green horse. He proposes a bargain whereby any one of the King's knights may strike off his head with the axe he carries providing that the same knight will accept a return blow in a year's time. Gawaine takes up the challenge and is astonished to see the Green Knight pick up his head after being decapitated, order Gawaine to meet him at the Green Chapel at the stipulated time, and then gallop off with his head under his arm.

The next Christmas sees Gawaine in a vast and dreary forest looking for the Green Chapel. The lord of a nearby castle offers him hospitality for the remaining days before his rendezvous, telling his that the chapel in question is only a few miles distant. The lord also makes a stipulation: he will go hunting each day while Gawaine remains at the castle with his wife. At the end of each day, they will exchange their spoils.

While the lord is out hunting, however, his lovely wife comes into Gawaine's room and tries to seduce him. Our knight, conscious of duty and honour toward his host, will do no more than let her kiss him. When the lord comes back and presents the venison he has caught to Gawaine, the latter gives him a kiss, his "spoils" for that day.

The second day, the same thing happens, Gawaine trading another kiss for a boar. But, on the third day, the lady insists on giving him her green, golden-hemmed girdle, which this time Gawaine keeps secret, exchanging a third kiss for the fox that the lord has caught.

On the third day, Gawaine sets out for his appointed meeting and duly meets the Green Knight next to one of the chambered tombs known as 'barrows':

> It had a hole in each end and on either side,
> And was overgrown with grass in great patches.
> All hollow it was within, only an old cavern
> Or the crevice of an ancient crag...

True to the conditions, Gawaine lays his head upon the block – only for the giant to take two mock blows, which not unnaturally unnerve Gawaine somewhat.

Steeling himself to receive the third and fatal blow, he is exulted to feel the blade do no more than nick the side of his neck. Having fulfilled his promise and lived, he springs up joyfully to find that the Green Knight and his recent host are one and the same, and the cut he received at the third stroke was his punishment for stealing the girdle. The giant goes on to explain that his name is Bertilak of the High Desert, and that the lady in his castle is none other than Morgan le Fay, Gawaine's aunt. The whole adventure has been a magical test, not only for himself as an individual, but also for the spirit behind the whole Round Table.

Now, like a Sufi tale, the true meaning of this is a secret between God and the individual interpretation of each reader. But, in broad terms, we can catch glimpses within this story of the head-cult that was common throughout Celtic society, of solar heroes, fertility rites – all spiced up with Troubadour ethics of courtly love.

But, underneath these glimpses, we can find the enduring image of Osiris in his aspect of Vegetation God, as the Corn King losing his head to be born again next year. The Green Knight is the cyclical aspect of Nature, or death and renewal, but he is also Osiris challenging Horus and testing his worthiness to succeed him. There are the Osirian parallels of the dwelling mound, the desert land in which he lives, the girdle (which represents the *tat*, or 'girdle' of Isis) the axe which parallels the adze (an image of the constellation of the Great Bear) that Horus used for the ceremony of the Opening of the Mouth that caused fertility to burst forth once more.

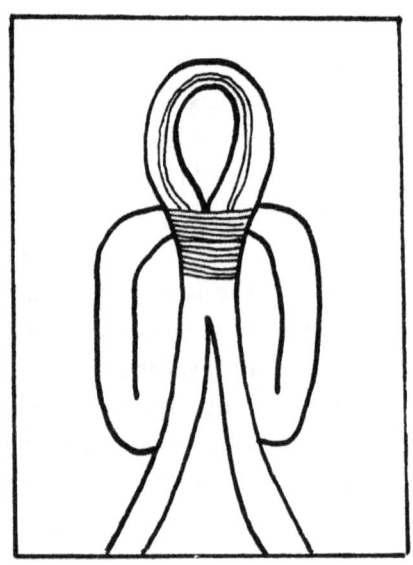

*The tat (buckle or knot of Isis)*

As regards that girdle/garter, there is also William Gray's comment relating to Venus, the planet of Love:

> To control Venus, the secret of her Zona, or girdle, had to be known. It was tied with a special knot, and its pattern hid the secret. Once this was mastered, Love came under control of Will, for the knot could be fastened or unfastened according to the Initiate's intention.[17]

As Ankh-f-n-Khonsu said: "Love is the law, love under will."

We shall return to Lancelot and Gawaine later, and in more ways than one, for they are the Celtic images of the New Aeon under whose aegis we might learn to work. They are levels of consciousness which we can choose to explore within ourselves and thus stimulate similar levels in the consciousness of humanity as a whole. But first we must press on to that final part within the Arthurian Cycle in which his role as Priest-King gives way to his inevitable glory as Sacrificed God.

The basic events are simple enough. Arthur's bastard son, Mordred, comes to Camelot and takes his place in court. At the Feast of Pentecost, a marvellous vision of the Holy Grail appears before the Knights of the Round Table. This vessel was widely regarded as the cup out of which Christ drank at the Last Supper, but which has many echoes of Celtic cauldron myths from earlier periods. In itself, the vision turns the feast into something of a Last Supper also, for all the knights then depart in quest of the Grail. But someone should have warned them; they should never have gone. It was the effective end of order within the court.

The Round Table begins to fall apart. Gradually, Mordred engineers things so that Arthur is forced to admit that he has been 'given the horns', as was once said – cuckolded by his best friend. Lancelot is caught in bed with the Queen, but manages to flee the trap.

Guinevere is brought to trial and found guilty under Arthur's own laws. As she is about to be burnt to death, Lancelot mounts a rescue and carries her off to Bamburgh. Eventually Guinevere goes back to Arthur of her own accord, but the King lays siege to his former champion's castle. Meanwhile, Guinevere is then abducted by Mordred, who proclaims himself as King.

---

17 William G. Gray, *The Ladder of Lights*. (Toddington, UK: Helios, 1968), p. 81.

Arthur withdraws his troops from Bamburgh and pursues Mordred's army.

Finally, at the battle of Camlann, the two armies wipe each other out, and the mortally wounded King is helped to the shore of a lake by Sir Bedivere. After some persuasion, Sir Bedivere throws the sword Excalibur out into the lake, where a lady's arm rises as before and takes it to its proper place. Arthur, mortally wounded, is last seen carried off in a magic barge, attended by three Queens, on his journey to the mystic Isle of Avalon. There he waits, not dead but not really alive, until the time comes when Britain faces deadly peril again…

That is a bare retelling of some of the most poignant events in literary history, but it will do for a start. Let us look at some of the more esoteric aspects now.

Mordred was a bastard. The bastard son of Arthur by his half-sister Morgan le Fay, the Witch-Queen of the Britons and Bretons. Morgan, as noted, used her magical powers to trick her step-brother into sleeping with her, which immediately gives her a link with Nephthys in her Celtic aspect. As stepsister to Arthur, her mating corresponds directly to those between the pharaoh and his sister, the intention being the preservation or strengthening of a sacred blood-line. Mordred, it was hoped, would be a Wonderchild just as his father had been.

Magicians almost uniformly agree that Morgan (sometimes said to mean 'sea-born') was the title given to a high priestess of Atlantean origin, the direct counterpart of the Merlin. This is the sea-priestess who came to the western shores in order to teach men the ways of the Moon, the powers of the sea, and the secrets of sacred bloodlines.

Now this 'occult eugenics' or selective breeding is something repugnant to us today – in part because of those energies released by Guinevere – but in an Aeon when humanity was by no means as individuated as now, when communities had a much more herd-like collective consciousness, these practices were a means of making links with evolutionary energies on inner levels. In time, via the nature of those Sacred Kings who used and understood these energies, the benefit was passed on to the people as a whole.

The cycle contains one long story in which Morgan manages to steal the scabbard of Excalibur from the King for a brief while.

Beneath the Christian gloss of these tales, and determined attempts to give Morgan some purely evil attributes, we can find within this act traces of a struggle between the patriarchal systems which eventually dominated the West and those Mysteries of Women which they superseded.

Morgan wanted the healing scabbard because, as a woman, it was hers by right, and because she found herself fighting a Kingship that had lost its balance and thus tried to appropriate everything to the masculine. The scabbard was the talisman of the proto-witches; healing was their province, their magic. But an unbalanced masculinity was trying to keep it for its sole use, aided and abetted by a Christian Church which found the idea of any kind of fertility cult pure anathema. Hence the Christian scribe/interpreter's insistence that the winners of the Grail were chaste virgins.

Ridiculous as it may sound, this was a little notion which survived the centuries, so that magicians and occultists of all persuasions, even until comparatively recent decades, remained convinced that spiritual attainment was proportionate to sexual abstinence. Although that was one attitude Ankh-f-n-Khonsu never shared. No one was going to make *him* keep his pants on. And in many curious ways, he helped smooth the way for witches of today to reclaim that inner talisman of the scabbard and to use it in its proper manner. All this came about because of the battles fought by Morgan and her kind upon the outer and the inner planes.

I grew up on the writings of Blavatsky, Annie Besant, A.P. Sinnet, C.W. Leadbeater, Alice Bailey and a host of others. As a teenager, their insistence on the need for chastity troubled me deeply. They were High Initiates, Adepts, bringing through teachings from the Masters. They could not be wrong could they?

I asked William G. Gray, an Adept himself, what he thought of all this. He instantly banished all such nonsense with a simple sentence in one his many letters to me which began: "Balls to Alice Bailey the pompous old prude..."

Her son Mordred, on the other hand, is what might be termed a Triple God figure. The others in his trinity would be Lancelot and Gawaine. Being son and nephew to the King, his very birth was attended by portents.

Merlin had prophesied that Arthur would be killed by a person born on Mayday, the ancient Celtic feast of Beltain. And so the King ordered all children born of nobility on the day in question to be put to death. The method of execution involved putting the babes on board a ship and sending it to sea and certain shipwreck. When the inevitable happened, Mordred was the only survivor, being washed ashore where he was found and looked after by a good man. There are obvious Biblical echoes here, and we are reminded too of the Welsh bard Taliesin being set adrift in a coracle. Much the same as happened to Anubis, too.

In some ways Mordred is like Set; he was the victim of a bad press. Mordred is that energy which stops a man becoming set in his ways. Or: Mordred is that energy which stops a man from becoming Set in his ways. It is a play upon words, but there is wisdom to be gleaned from it nevertheless.

In one sense, Mordred aptly fits into the role of Lord of Justice – a British Thoth in balance with the Hermes and Anubis of Gawaine and Lancelot, respectively. Although, like all Triple Gods, the qualities can change like alternating currents. But the Set comparison is more appropriate in the way that he challenges Arthur for the Kingship, much as Set challenged first Osiris and then Horus for the same.

In some tales, it is Mordred who elopes with Guinevere in an act of mutual complicity. In these tales, he is far removed from the malignant and cowardly traitor that the popular imagination casts him as being. What we must realize is that Osiris (and thus Everyman) actually becomes Set when he tries to hang onto his power. Women are best able to understand this. A woman loses a peculiar type and quality of power – her fertility – during the menopause, and then must learn to seek a different kind of fertility, and one which is not related to bearing children. It is not a fate that afflicts man's sperm, obviously, but he too must learn to give way, and let go, in completely different areas.

The temporal power of the male over his own realm does not necessarily have to become corrupt – there are ways to avoid this –

but it always becomes corrupt when he seeks to perpetuate this power for the length of his days. There are things man must learn to yield to, not least of which are the needs of his wife and children – who are growing just as much as he. The times when this yielding is most appropriate must also be learned. Like the Osirian corn-dollies, with barley pushing up through the framework, all men must allow their dependants to grow through them, and glorify him in that way.

Mordred understood that. In magical terms, his is the disruptive energy which perpetually breaks up and destroys all forms. He breaks up and destroys – but he also sets free. He also Sets free. These acts of destruction, when performed by a Sacrificial Priest, can produce energy which will, as Dion Fortune says in *The Sea Priestess*, 're-appear on the planes of form as an entirely different type of force to that as which it started.' So the power behind the Arthurian Cycle – power which was in danger of being ossified through its complacency – was actually transmuted by Mordred and then stored until the day it would be needed again. He destroyed the old order based upon the sort of 'selective breeding' that was valid for that time and type of consciousness. This is all too appallingly reminiscent of the Nazi *Lebensborn* program, which included human stud farms aimed at creating a super race. He destroyed this order by bringing out into the open those energies flowing through Guinevere, whom he helps to balance.

Mordred, Gawaine and Lancelot are, then, aspects of one type of energy perhaps best associated with the planet Mars, in astrological terms. They counter-balance the trinity of Guinevere, Morgan le Fay, and Elaine (associated with the planet Jupiter). The Triple God and these Three Queens form what we might think of as the two wings of the Dragon. Within them are to be the qualities which will enable the serpent-powers to uncoil themselves and rise up from their abode – whether this is in the Tuat, the underground cave, or that chakra at the base of the spine associated with the kundalini. Through them the serpent energies are given both lift and direction; with wings, the serpent becomes a dragon and can fly. It is a rising and a flight based upon an interchange of energies for which sexual union is a low level analogue and also a primary key.

It is the sort of interchange hinted at, in crude form, by the exchange of gifts between Gawaine and the Green Knight. These are the energies involved in working with Ankh-f-n-Khonsu's famous dictum 'Love is the law, Love under will', which in itself prevents his 'Do what thou wilt shall be the whole of the Law' from being solely an expression of Might is Right.

Before we go on to completely new fields, we might take one final look at the concept of Guinevere from the Egyptian viewpoint and so tie up some loose ends in this comparative mythology.

The clearest parallel to her can be found in the image of Hathor, whose role oscillates between that of Isis, as protectress and defender of women's rights, and Sekhmet, the lioness deity who cannot be appeased once she has tasted blood. Hathor's name is derived from Het-Hert, Het-Heru, Hwt-Hert or Hethara, meaning House of Horus. In hieroglyphs, her name is drawn as a large enclosure with a Horus falcon within. In this aspect she was seen as the great sky itself, holding Horus within her womb, which was poetically referred to as 'house'.

Although it is rarely appropriate to think in linear terms for these deities, there are indications that she was older than any of the deities in the Heliopolitan Recension. Her many titles include: Lady of the Sycamore Tree, Lady of the West, Lady of the Stars and the Golden One. She was the very incarnation of dance and sexuality. Not only was she known as the Lady of the Vulva but she also had the epithet 'Hand of God', which was a reference to masturbation. One myth tells of how Ra had become so depressed that he refused to speak to anyone. Hathor, who never suffered depression or doubt, danced before him and exposed her private parts, which caused him to laugh out loud and shine again.

Call me old fashioned, call me vulgar, but I can't help liking a goddess of this nature. She had (has) a sense of horny fun.

In later stages of her cult, it was customary for the Queen of Egypt to identify herself with Hathor and lead the other priestesses in the temple rituals devoted to Horus and the other gods. She was the goddess of music, art, dancing and all light-hearted pleasures. Plus she was the Goddess of Love – that most of all. The Troubadours, railing against a time when the masculine had for too long been exalted at the expense of the feminine, would have adored her.

Because of her natural connections with fertility, Hathor often overlapped with Isis as regards the rising of the Nile and the Dog-star,

Sothis. She is indeed the Horned Goddess, the Lady of the Sycamore Tree which some traditions insist was the tree that grew up around Osiris' body after it had been washed ashore at Byblos. She was the goddess who suckled dead souls, and in the Late Period while a dead man was still called an Osiris, dead women were Hathors – which again shows that these names were as much titles or descriptions of function as anything personal.

> Hathor was represented as a star-spangled cow, as a woman with a broad human or sistrum-shaped head and cow's ears or wearing a solar disk between the horns. She is most often seen with a sistrum as goddess of joy; suckling the living or dead; or as Goddess of the West, standing on the mountain of the West to welcome the dying sun into her arms – a combination of her solar and Osirian characteristics.[18]

I think (know) the archetypes can also make unexpected appearances in both animal and human form, although the witness usually doesn't realise it until they have gone.

Some years ago I stood on the smaller barrow atop Cley Hill, swaying into my trance and the song of the earth and trying to find my totem beast – whatever it would be – when I was knocked off my feet by the amiable charge of a young cow, butting into the small of my back. "Christ!" I swore, on that most pagan of heights, before turning to see a creature as startled as myself, quivering but holding its ground. *Touch it* said a voice within, and I did, gently, its wet snout, and the link was made.

Now my robust and wonderful ego, my conscious mind, had hoped for something like a fox, hare, black dog or stag – something traditional and reasonably magnificent – and at first I was arrogant enough to be disappointed. But in the light of my own life, nature and direction, this creature was perfect. A horned sending from the horned deity who presided over the place.

And a human analogue or manifestation of Hathor appeared during the bleakest time of my life when I wore very large and painful horns of my own, felt unloved and unlovable, unfancied and unwanted, with no worthwhile future, and found myself living in a place called

---

18 Ions, *op. cit.*, p. 82.

Sycamore Grove. A woman appeared in my life called Heather, who loved music, art, dancing and all light-hearted pleasures. Even her last name, as I only realised long after she had gone, was exquisitely apt.

The relationship was never going to last but she gave me the warmth, self-esteem, sex and support that I needed to put myself back together. Soon, she made me whole. I could fly again.

As we lay in bed one night I noted that her long black hair, shot with silver, covered prominent, strangely-shaped ears and I wondered where I had seen these before. It was only later, when she had moved on and far away that I saw a picture of Hathor from the temple columns of Denderah, and remembered.

Did Heather think of herself as a manifestation of Hathor? I doubt it: she was a Quaker.

I never worshipped her, as I tended to do with all my loves, but she had my complete respect.

In another world, another time, another stratum of consciousness, the Horned Gods of Europe would have recognised her as their own true consort. As our imagination flickers back and forth between the images of Gwenhwyfar and Hathor, one charging up the other in a kind of synergistic exchange, we can see how she can cross both worlds and both times as the Lady of the Sycamore – a title that could have come from any of the witch-cults. If the Horned God of the West, who is the true subject of this book, can be seen to ride from the darkness between the trees (that fecund darkness within which the seeds of life and light germinate), then she is to be found within the trees themselves, emanating love and law – or *maat*. Soon, we will learn to talk with her. This, really, is all her husband has ever wanted us to do …

# THE CAVES AND FORESTS

The Horned God comes from the darkness – that curious, living, intensely aware darkness which exists within the forest, between the trees, and through which the shafts of light roar down to form the columns of some great arboreal cathedral. The Horned God, who is of course the presiding deity within this cathedral, was well-known to the early Celts who made their homes on the edge of those vast forests that once covered most of Europe – and most of the world.

We find him in Rheims, where an image survives which shows him holding a large bag from which pours a stream of coins, while below him lurk a bull and a stag. These figures might be regarded as his true courtiers. We find him in Paris, on the Pilier des Nautes, where his upper body has survived on otherwise damaged stonework. This shows him with upward pointing horns, from each of which hangs a torc. He also has two pairs of ears – one human and the other animal.

On the Gundestrup cauldron, which can be seen in the National Museum at Copenhagen, he is seen with his splendid antlers, surrounded by wild beasts which include a wolf and a stag. He is also holding a ram-headed serpent in his left hand. In a similar vein, on a cross-shaft at Clonmacnois in Ireland, he is portrayed grasping two wolves by their tails.

At Val Camonica in Italy, on a very old rock carving indeed, he is shown as a tall standing figure with antlers and what may be torcs – symbols of authority – on his arms.

On a small plaque in the Corinium Museum at Cirencester in England he is shown holding a serpent in each hand. A similar bronze figure was found in the same region at Southbroom in Wiltshire, where the God is standing and again holds ram-headed serpents, which coil around his legs.

And there is a Pictish carving from Meigle in Perthshire, Scotland, which depicts a horned deity holding an intricate pattern of coils derived from a pair of serpents and with coiling legs ending in fish-tails. Even to the most sober and non-mystical commentator:

> The Celts clearly saw him as an earth god of fertility and plenty. The snake symbolizes the life-force and powers of regeneration, hence its representation on the staff of Aesculapius and the caduceus of Mercury. It is only in the Garden of Eden that the serpent became evil.[19]

But perhaps the first known representation is within the Caverne des Trois Frères in the Ariege, which some sources estimate dates back 30,000 years or more. To call this particular image a Horned God, however, is something of a misnomer in this instance because it is clearly a man clothed in the skin of a stag, and wearing its antlers, so that his whole body is covered by the animal's hide. His head and feet are clearly seen as though the material were transparent. So it is obviously the intention of the artist, working in an awkward and difficult part of the cave, to show us a priest fully possessed by his God.

Another image, from the Fourneau du Diable, the figure is shown not only dancing, but also accompanying himself with an instrument variously described as a kind of musical bow or even a flute. Decide for yourself. In all cases these images indicate a time when the priesthood and its priestesses would invoke their totemic spirits with the help of ritual masks.

---

19 Graham Webster, *The British Celts and their Gods under Rome.* (London: Batsford, 1986).

••• the caves and forests •••

Now this is not "primitive" magic, but rather a technique that was used consistently throughout the Egyptian Mysteries, and within many of those religions and cults that sprang up around the Mediterranean.

There is a temple painting from Denderah which shows a priest wearing the mask of Anubis being led to a religious ceremony. The use of masks in Greek and Roman ritual dramas is well documented, while at the other side of the known world masks were vital to those Mysteries of Mithras practiced throughout Roman Britain. Indeed, within the ruined Temple of Mithras at Carrawburgh, along Hadrian's Wall, it is still possible to catch disconcerting glimpses of the astral forms of those officiants who took their places within the niches along each wall – each one resplendent in the appropriate human or animal mask.

**As I look back upon my life as it flows around my calm Zen garden, and try to rake it into shape, I realise that I have never been obsessed by the notion of past lives. Of course I have had various inner 'pulses' (memories is not quite the right term) which seem to indicate connections with Lindisfarne, Egypt and Roman Britain. But whether these are disparate aspects of my Higher Self; 'other' lives, in which everything is happening simultaneously; fragments of some great hologram; or actual previous lives in the traditional sense... I really do not know. Sometimes, for the sake of simple discussion, it is better to act 'as if' the latter were the case.**

So the Mithraeum at Carrawburgh has always been one of my own holy places. When I was a boy of about 8, going on a coach trip with a group of elderly blind people to a place called Talkin Tarn, the rattling old bus heaved across the Northumbrian moors. With my Mam and blind grandad behind me, I had a double seat to myself and I used the space to play with my plastic Roman soldiers.

Although the bus never stopped, my attention was suddenly gripped by a lonely signpost simply marked: 'Temple of Mithras.' It pointed to the left, across bleak fields and toward distant hills, and although I bashed my head against the window in my urge to see, there was nothing visible. I had no revelations, no visions, but it set off a kind of 'tone' within me that was utterly familiar yet completely new. If anything, I felt a kind of dumb, hurt surprise that such a place was pointed out like that for everyone to see. I knew that one day, when I was a big boy, I would have to come back.

I suppose that some part of me might have been a Priest of Mithras who spent some little time along Hadrian's Wall before being slaughtered by a particularly angry Pict. How much of this is genuine 'far memory' or a piece of unconscious story-telling to make things fit – I do not know. Although this priest would have taken on the role and worn the mask of the Raven, I don't think he was much more than a civil servant, concerned with administrative rather than occult matters. In those days you had to be 'belong' to the cultus if you were to get anywhere in the Roman Army, just as in the early 20$^{th}$ Century membership of Freemasonry was a prime requisite for the ambitious.

Christine Hartley told me that this was one of her own holy places too. Despite the apparently all-male emphasis of the Mithraic Mysteries, there was also a 'Nymphaeum', a shrine to local water nymphs, at the site. I met a woman once in the Savoy Hotel who I'm quite certain once served as a priestess there, but I got a huge, 'keep away' injunction in my head and so I did.

Further afield still, among the Native Americans, we find wooden masks representing simple elemental forces such as the Spirit of the Wind, or Cold Weather. The Kwakuitl tribes of British Columbia created sophisticated masks. These incorporated mechanical devices through which the shaman could give himself a new face during the ritual dances, and create the maximum effect.

··· the caves and forests ···

*Egyptian priest wearing the jackal mask*

We could posit several major masks within the natural realm: the Mask of the Raven, associated with Saturn; the Mask of the Dove, which relates to Jupiter; that of the Hawk, which can be used to invoke the forces of Mars. Then there is the Mask of the Royal Stag of the Sun, on whose antlers birds perch; the Cow (or Bull) of Venus; the Mask of the Fox, for Mercury; the Mask of the Hare of the Moon and the Mask of the Earth Serpent. These represent a broad spectrum of consciousness that can be tapped with the aid of the tutelary deities concerned. These deities are, in a sense, the Higher Aspects of familiars beloved by witches.

Sometimes, instead of masks, suggestive symbols were used – black feathers in the hair, pelts, antlered helmets – all of these were backed up by the vitality of natural locations, huge fires, light from the heavens, songs, chants, clapping, and drums – those great drums that can make the earth shake and force you to follow their beat no matter what. But in each case the real work was done by the actual human who was channelling these forces – male or female. Great actors and mime artists have an uncanny talent for becoming greater than themselves, projecting such semi-illusions not solely by mere technique but by the inner assumption of animal 'essence.'

In this sanitized world, we have too easily chosen to ignore or scorn the effect of masks. In the negative sense, they can create an air of maliciousness and menace to make even the puniest villains seem filled with power. Masks obliterate the human personality with all its frail quirks, all its physiological imperfections. Made properly and used with skill on highly charged occasions, the effect upon the consciousness of the celebrants can be staggering. Holes can be punched in the rational defences, and the candidate for initiation can be made to know that he is, beyond any doubt, in the company of gods. From the operator's point of view, masks can, by subduing the vitally important sense of smell, create the sense that what is being seen is not truly three-dimensional, not truly happening to the mundane personality at all. By suppressing the impact of one dimension, masks allow the interaction with other dimensions in its place.

In the bright and holy stillness of my garden that all seems quite sinister now, yet it is true enough. Christine Hartley told me that when she worked magic within the Amoun Temple of the Golden Dawn, masks were used with extraordinary effect. I think it was Crowley – or was it Yeats? – who lamented that when the Golden Dawn stopped using masks, the rituals lost something. I was also present when the late Murry Hope donned a cat-like mask to take a group on a shamanic journey which several people in the audience found disturbing and had to leave. Mind you Murry herself, god bless her, was so beautifully feline that the mask was hardly necessary in her case. She was a real changeling.

I have never used masks myself, though I suppose the technique known as the Assumption of the God-form is a true equivalent, in which I visualise myself in the form of say Anubis, or Herne, and work myself inward and upward to try and become him. Some time ago when about to give a lecture on Cernunnos, in Seattle, I did this and as I walked up to the lecture room from the basement my deeply-psychic host commented wryly: "Gee, I like your hat!"

And recently I was compelled to spend some time before I visited the First World War battlefields around Ypres absorbing all I could about General Haig. Having spent a year among the dead writing my odd *Geordie's War* I felt certain that I would meet lost, trapped souls over there. They wouldn't listen to me, Little Alan, but Haig had the authority to get through to them. So on a grey, drizzling day, before that pitiful and yet pitiless mound known as Hill 60, I assumed Haig's features, his attitude, stance and his uniform – all in as much detail as I could – in order to 'become' him, before calling on the wraiths there to Stand To. A handful came: earthbound Tommies and one somewhat wary Fritz. I told them in clipped tones that the war was over, that they had done their duty – and right well – and that they could now Stand Down and enter the Light behind them, and go home...

I think they did: in the No Man's Land of my own mind at very least.

We have already noted Osiris' role as a Horned God and seen how his qualities were vital to the theocratic culture of Egypt over enormous periods of time. In other cult centres along the Nile it was Amun, originally a local deity of Thebes, who took on the Osirian head-gear in this respect. Generally, the goddesses wore the horns of cattle while the gods were adorned with the horns of sheep or rams. Thus a priest of Amun would wear the curved horns of the Theban ram and ram's skin over his shoulders in much the same way that the dancing man of the Ariege was wrapped within skins of his own. Far from being the 'primitive' religious expression of a hunting/gathering Stone Age culture, this assumption of animal forms, in one way or another, was fundamental to the deepest practices of all cultures at that time.

But I would go a step further and predict that occult historians in a century's time will look back upon this decade as the moment when the scattered parts of the dismembered Western Mystery Tradition were finally reconstructed, all save one piece. When that piece is found (and it will be soon), when the shaman/animist elements make their necessary and transforming return to the Tradition, then it will twitch into real life once more. This will be the moment when Osiris, the Horned God, will be given back his balls.

I stand by that, though I'm not sure it will be an entirely peaceful process. There will be a lot more chaos before it all calms down. I do look forward to a time when priests and priestesses will actually have power again, instead of merely the ability to make noises. In this wise I was long ago struck by the words of Evan John Jones:

> ...there is only one way of finding a Witch: judge them by their works and by their silence – unless there is a need to speak out. If one who claims to be

a Witch can perform the tasks of Witchcraft, i.e. summon the spirits and they come, can divine with rod, fingers and birds. If they can also claim the right to the omens and have them; have the power to call, heal and curse and above all, can tell the maze and cross the Lethe, then you have a witch.[20]

John Jones was a very simple man who wouldn't have known his Atziluth from his Briah, but he could do all of the above and more. When I grow up, I want to be like him.

I want the same or similar for the modern magicians but instead they get hung up on arguing whether someone was a 7=4 when they were clearly a mere 4=7, and whether someone's 5=6 was even valid, given the fact they had their fingers crossed during the entire initiation.

The Horned God was found in bull form, for example, during the Bronze and Iron Ages around the Aegean Sea, where we can find the legend of the Minotaur of Crete and see a human wearing a bull's head and horns being worshipped with dance and sacrifice. This Minotaur was held to be the sacred offspring of the Cretan queen, who appeared robed and masked as a cow, and who was mated with a foreign 'bull' at regular ritual intervals. This is also tied up with the image and concept of ritual sacrifice discussed below.

And then there was Pan. There is always Pan. With his long, narrow face, small horns, and goat's legs, he is first cousin to the dancing god shown earlier.[21]

Pan and his ilk are directly comparable to the Aker, that 'part man part beast' who guards the portals of the Underworld, and who can usher us into the mysteries of the natural realm with which it overlaps.

This is true of the Horned God and his consort generally. Their concerns are with the Land (and its parallels in human consciousness) and what lies below it (and the parallels therein, too). The Horned

---

20 Quoted from my own *Inner Guide to the Megaliths*, Immanion Press 2012.
21 The magician C. R. F. Seymour commented '... these 'conductors of the dead' are also in many cases the instigators of the teachings of the Mysteries. Their role of 'Walker of Two Worlds' made them the guardian of neophyte and initiate alike ...'

# the caves and forests

*Horned Gods guarding the gate of the Underworld*

God, however he manifests himself, can be approached on a number of levels in much the same way that the simple faun, who was Pan of Arcady, came to take on levels of sophistication that the original worshippers may not have recognized or understood.

A common link between priests of different religions and cultures would have been the animal forms used in their mysteries, and the symbols which best represented their deities. They would have been able to discuss their totemic beasts in much the same way that people today can ask: "What sort of car do you have?" – which in itself can pass on trivial clues as to status and self-image. Arm-bands, made of the feathers, fur or teeth of the bird or beast in question, were symbols of the priest's allegiance, and these later became – for security reasons – transformed into garters which could be hidden on the leg, under clothing.

It was only when the Romans began to conquer Europe that we begin to pick up written records of the gods they encountered, even though these were often described in terms of their own state religion. Even so, as soldiers who followed the fighting man's Cult of Mithras (which may well have overtaken Christianity had it made some appeal to women), they would have seen in the local Horned Gods clear echoes of the Sacred Bull so central to their own initiation ceremonies. Indeed, the ritual slaughter of the Mithraic 'Bull of the Sun,' in whose blood the initiates were soaked, may well have been a direct descendant of the Osirian slaying of the Apis Bull, which in itself was held to be an incarnation of the Horned God, Osiris, himself.

In fact we can see within this the conceptual elements of sacrifice as 'going down through the worlds,' in a manner of speaking. First, there was the willing sacrifice of humans. Then, when humanity outgrew this need, it was animals. Today, in the Christian church, we can find an expression of what might be called vegetable sacrifice during the English Harvest Festival, when produce is offered up on the altar. The mineral sacrifice is part of a mystery still to come.

**I'm being portentous again, with that last. Yet I also think it is true. Just don't ask for details. Not yet.**

So, to get back to our theme, it was through the Romans that we can begin to pick up Cernunnos. The word itself is Latinized Celtic, found inscribed on the altar which lay under the Christian altar of the Cathedral of Notre Dame in Paris. The name simply means 'Horned One,' or even 'Old Hornie.'

> The name appears in every variation throughout the area of Indo-European speech. The chief god of the Fertility Cult in Ireland was (and is still) known as Conall Cernac. His name is enshrined in both English "Cornwall" and Breton 'Kerne' (the French 'Cornouaille').[22]

It is generally held that the shrine of Cern in Paris was 'rehabilitated' by being overlaid with the new faith of Christianity, but this was not always the case. Sometimes places of power, which were also places of worship, just came to the end of their useful life as far as the original energies went. This might be compared to a battery going flat. Rightly or wrongly, the Christianity of the time simply recharged each place, tapping those forces which lay beneath, but in a different way and at a different frequency. It was not always a simple matter of one faith obliterating another. At least not in the earliest days, when

---

22 Michael Harrison, *The Roots of Witchcraft* (London: Muller, 1973), p. 84.

## the caves and forests

Christians still knew how to work with power. The overlying of the original altar in this case was not an instance of religious conquest and suppression, but a sacramental act which acknowledged that which had gone before.

Some of the ancient churches in my area today, most of them clearly built on top of ancient pagan sites, are replete with spiritual energies. One little chapel was always happy for me to put astral images of Isis and Osiris into empty niches at either side of the altar and work accordingly.

Another seemed to growl at me whenever I walked through the door with visitors – who usually adored the place.

Yet another was calm, dull and quiescent until my wife and I quietly said the Paternoster and it suddenly came alive as if recognising the Old Language of centuries gone. We are not Catholics, I hasten to add, nor Esoteric Christians nor yet hardened Pagans. I don't think Light concerns itself too much about such modern fads.

The same God, Cern, can be found in Brittany. This is a region that has never regarded itself as being French, and which is wrapped up in the figure of Saint Cornely. This saint is an imaginary pope said to have been martyred in 253 A.D. – a fate which is peculiarly appropriate as far as Horned Gods are concerned. He is the patron saint of horned beasts and he is always depicted in church statuary and banners in the company of a bull. His name comes from the old Gaulish word for 'horn,' which is a potent symbol that is outwardly male, but inwardly female. The snake swallowing its own tail manages to convey the same concept of male and female conjoined in one body. It is perhaps because of this idea that snakes are often depicted along with Cernunnos.

We can find him again on the other side of the Channel – almost directly opposite in Cerne Abbas, Dorset, Where in Anglo-Saxon times a large monastic foundation grew up on the site of a shrine. Here, carved on the chalk hillside above the site, the massive club-

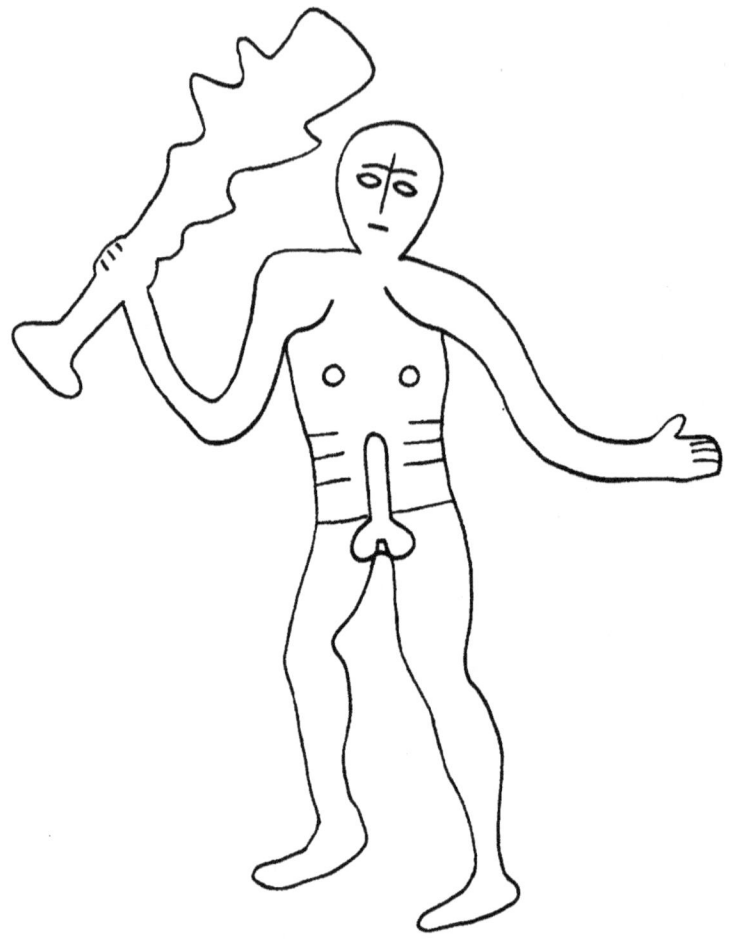

*The Cerne Abbas hill carving*

wielding giant still rules supreme. The Christian monastery came and went, but the old God still remains, no longer horned but clearly 'horny'.[23]

Although the word 'cerne' is invariably pronounced with a soft c today (thus "Sern Abbas"), it is recognized that 'kern' is the older and more accurate pronunciation. However, I would go one further and

---

[23] And he can be found in Cern, in Switzerland, in a completely different way, where the multi-national research physicists accelerate pencil-sized beams of sub-atomic electrons and positrons to all but the speed of light in opposite directions around a 16-mile circular tunnel. Those particles, crashing together, produce energy of the intensity matched only in the first millisecond of the original Big Bang which created the universe in the first place.

••• the caves and forests •••

suggest that it should be pronounced with the sort of rasp that should be given to the *ch* in the Scottish word loch, or lake. It is the anaemic English attempt to say 'Cern' in its proper manner which has resulted in him being called 'Herne', for the sake of the tonsils.

The Cerne giant, then, was once regarded as a wondrous source of fertility. Barren women had only to sit upon him – ideally on the phallus itself – in order to become fertile; although most people felt that it was more effective for a husband and wife to have full intercourse there to cure the same problem. The giant was, and is, not just a chalk carving on a hillside, but a key that could unlock fertilities within those who approached him properly. In the small enclosure above his head, known today as the Frying Pan, a maypole was said to have been erected annually for the May Day celebrations, which were in themselves descendants of those great pre-Christian feasts of Beltaine. Wherever the maypole was really erected, whether in Cerne or anywhere else, we have a superb and obvious symbol of the Earth God becoming hard for the benefit of his people. Quite literally, by means of the coloured cords radiating from the tip of the pole, and onto which the dancers held, the people bound themselves to him.

Our old friend Geb would have been at home in Cerne Abbas, where the erect giant can still be seen sprawled across the earth below the arching sky.

So in various ways and for various reasons the Horned God's worship co-existed with Christianity long enough to reach that era when details of his priesthood began to be written down; even though this was invariably done from a jaundiced viewpoint, and from one in which any God other than Jesus or Jehovah was necessarily the very manifestation of Darkness. A few examples have survived, however, and these are worth looking at.

There was Suibhne (Sweeney) Gelt, King of the Dal Araidhe in Northern Ireland, who went mad after the major battle of Magh Rath in 642 A.D. He then wandered desolate regions, often showing evidence of supernatural powers. These included the ability to ride upon a fawn and exert control over the wild stags of his bleak world. Indeed, he had a herd of stags which he used to pull ploughs – a hint of the old deities of agriculture working under the aegis of the Stag God. Suibhne Gelt was so identified with stags, in fact, that he was emphatically described as being a herbivore, or more poetically a "tongue of the wild land," made to crawl among cresses.

Then comes the Black Man, from the Romance of Owain, who was:

> ... as large as two ordinary men; he has but one foot, and one eye in the middle of his forehead. And he has a club of iron, and certainly there are no two men in the world who could bear that club. And he is no handsome man, but on the contrary exceedingly ugly; and he is the ranger of the wood. And you will see a thousand wild animals grazing around him.[24]

As Owain later said, with awe, the animals 'bowed their heads, and did him homage as their Lord.' The term 'ranger of the wood' and his general role as something of a guardian and protector, points to the fact that specific areas, such as woods, mountains, lakes, and so on, very often have entities associated with them which, for lack of a better term, we might simply describe as 'lesser gods'.

At least that is how they would have been regarded in earlier times. Thus a particular area, and every creature living within it, would fall under the aegis of something or someone akin to Owain's extraordinary Black Man. Once, on a bitter and pure winter's day in Wisconsin, I made a tenuous and delightful contact with a young and half-awake entity that was entirely linked to a large pond, only waiting for the long days of the sun to come around again. But the Black Man in Owain's adventures was rather more than this. In fact, his blackness is a pure Osirian symbol – a reference to the silt, which covered his body when Isis first recovered it from the Nile – silt which in itself is a symbol replete with fertile associations. But it is in the single eye that we are made to consider him more carefully. Through that, we are thrown far beyond the more immediate and popular associations with the Cyclops of Greek mythology, and we find ourselves standing before the Heliopolitan mythology once more.

In that extraordinary battle which Horus had with Set, and which lasted as long as most mortals' lives, the hawk-god had his eye plucked out. This eye was given to Osiris by his son as a symbol of the confirmation of the new regime – the new order which had been established by his accession. The eye which remained was the Sun, and the one he lost was, in essence, the Moon.

---

24 Quoted by Nikolai Tolstoy in *The Quest for Merlin*, Hutchinson

••• the caves and forests •••

All of which is an indication of the sort of change in evolutionary consciousness we will discuss in due course.

This hearkens quite neatly on toward Norse mythology and the supreme figure of Odin. He gained his wisdom from beneath the famous ash tree, Yggdrasil, whose roots link the Underworld with the Heaven-World and which conceal an eagle, a squirrel, and four stags. Under these roots lay Mimir's Well. The wisdom of Mimir was only exchanged for the sacrifice of Odin's eye. And Odin, so the prophecies go, will one day be swallowed by the great wolf Fenris, who is none other than our friend Anubis again, in Northern guise.

This single-eye motif, then, is not one of deformity, but of knowledge. It is invariably linked with the concept of dominion over natural realms. The other eye, that which is lost or 'given' still exists within the Otherworld. There is an allusive (and elusive) reference here to the old Scottish Highland idea of a person having 'Two Sights' – one of the natural world and one of the realm beyond. But these single-eyed figures often come to us in dreams of a specific and highly peculiar kind.

Most dreams – the vast bulk of them – are little more than the water dripping down an overflow pipe. We can simply let them drain away. But we do occasionally get those which are meant to awaken us. These cyclopean dream-figures often occur during those times in a person's life when he or she is coming more surely under the shadow of the Horned God and his Lady. They might be regarded as signs of the awakening of particular brain-cells, and do not necessarily appear in our dreams to pass on specific information.

But these myths of Black Men and stag-herders apart, the high-water mark of Horned God descriptions is surely to be found in the *Vita Merlini* of Geoffrey of Monmouth, issued in 1150 A.D.

The Merlin of this book is far more primitive though no less appealing than the smooth and courtly figure so enduringly presented in the more popular Arthurian romances. Here he is shown as a true Lord of Stags, living alone in the woods with his favourite companions of the pig and the wolf. The deer, naturally, obey him.

He wears an antlered helmet. He eats as the deer eat. He has a wife/sister Gwendoloena. For a period of his life he was said to have gone mad and retreated into the wilderness, uttering prophecies about the world to come. Indeed, in one way or one level or another, this is something that happens to us all at some stage in our lives.

As mentioned earlier Joseph Campbell described the three phases as being Separation, Initiation and Return.

The Separation comes to us in the course of everyday life when, for reasons that are apparently beyond our control, our worlds fall apart, there is loneliness, savagery, and wilderness within us and around us; we have moods and experience feelings of such intensity and darkness that, in later years, we can only describe it as having gone through a kind of madness. This is the phase of Osiris Torn and Scattered, of du Lac's torment, and also the time of Merlin disintegrating into the forest.

It is only later that we find our own Initiations, and learn to begin again armed with the sudden conviction that we do, now, begin to understand some of the darker sides of life and can make our own predictions and interpolations accordingly.

This, of course, is an exceedingly mundane version of Merlin's experience, but one that is no less valid than others.

Now there are, necessarily, many Merlins, and many nations claiming him for their own. Nikolai Tolstoy, in his *The Quest for Merlin*, makes a brilliant case for his origins to be found on the Hart Fell, near the present-day town of Moffat, on the Scottish Border. To him Merlin was:

> ... the horned deity who watched over men and beasts, and received the souls of the departed into his habitation in the sky. He wore an antlered helm (probably deerskins as well), and in some degree acted out the part of the stag itself. His station was by a sacred spring on the edge of a mountain in the centre of the Caledonian Forest... A sacred apple tree or orchard grew nearby, and [he] was attended by animal familiars in the form of a pig and a wolf. The whole area of the mountain was regarded with awe and fear...[25]

But whether Merlin has the cervine qualities of Geoffrey of Monmouth's account, or the more political, King-making functions described by Thomas Malory and Robert de Boron (the Burgundian poet who also wrote about Joseph of Arimathea), his essential character remains the same – strong and often acid, roguish, insightful, capable

---

25 *Ibid.*, p. 86.

### ··· the caves and forests ···

of great flashes of anger and raw, truly magical power. But above all he is concerned for the people whose destinies he often guided.

The very name Merlin, of course, refers to 'a little bird', the name given to a small European falcon. In the present-day sport of falconry, which has even undergone a minor revival in recent times, the different sorts of hawks and their ideal human partners are still to be found listed as they were centuries before: a gerfalcon is for a king, a peregrine for an earl, a goshawk for a yeoman, sparrow-hawk for a priest, kestrel for a knave – and a merlin for a lady.

Another figure relating to our present theme is that of Lailoken, who first appeared in the 12th century Life of St. Kentigern, the patron saint of Glasgow. Lailoken was described as a madman who was kept at the court of King Rhydderch, rather like a resident shaman who often made startling prophecies. He had been driven mad during a battle fought along the banks of the River Liddel. In this battle, a host of warriors – dead souls – had appeared in the sky and accused Lailoken of having been responsible for all the slaughter. Tormented and driven by the voices within himself, he ran off into the forest where (like Suibhne Gelt, and for the same reasons) he lived the naked life of a wild man. In these tales, he is expressly identified with Merlin. Textual evidence also links him with the Myrddin of Welsh poetry, who is also unmistakably the Merlin of Geoffrey of Monmouth.

In all cases, we come across the same themes of wilderness and/or wasteland, control of beasts, the dissolution of the personality, and the ability to 'see' beyond this world. Looming over all these is the great bellowing image of the stag. In varying ways, all of these ideas are borne along by stags and linked with the concept of kings and kingship.

And then there is Gwyn ap Nudd, 'Light, Son of Darkness', of whom William G. Gray makes the comment:

> Actually 'Light, son of Darkness' signifies the old FIAT LUX, or the well-known Yang-Yin. It's just the old Celtic name for a Power of Eternal Alternation ... Almost anything could be expected of him. As Day came out of Night, Life came out of Death, Yes came out of No, and so creation continued ...
>
> In point of fact the whole damn thing developed out of what we now call shamanism. A sort of Nature Religion which arose from people's

personal experiences and reactions with Nature itself. This resulted in a response from specific humans causing a character-change that seemed to 'set them apart' from their ordinary fellows and 'make them special' so that they were considered to be priests or at least have what we now call Psi-powers, or uncommon faculties such as telepathy, clairvoyance, and possibly healing. Eventually it became noticed that this was becoming hereditary within familial lines. Once the connections had time to build up definite establishments and power-structures began ...

In time standard ceremonials were being handed down from one generation to another down the centuries, but at the back of everything the old spontaneous experience persisted ... In other words those who had 'attained' priesthood for several lives eventually got born with the knowledge and experience in their genes already so that the priesthood became an hereditary function.

However the ancestral memories of the early experiences have always been there, and humans have called them out in hopes of reviving the old links with ancient times so that it may be said in the old words of Adam: "My priesthood and my gift of prophecy shall He restore to me etc. ..." when speaking of the coming crucifixion.[26]

Make links with Gwyn, awaken impulses within the genes, and he will restore our potentials as priests and priestesses. Through him, we can initiate ourselves. Through his ancient vision, we can attempt to create new futures.

Like the very best of Horned Gods, not much is known about Gwyn. Students of popular folklore describe him as the Welsh Lord of the Faeries, which to the modern ear tends to give him simpering, tinkling, wimpish qualities. However, the modern idea of faeries as diminutive creatures is a condition somewhat akin to looking down the wrong end of a mytho-historical telescope. Faeries, fées, or fays was the common name for the original inhabitants of Europe.

> The faeries, then, were the descendants of the early people who inhabited northern Europe. They were pastoral but not nomad, they lived in the un-forested parts of the country where there was good pasturage for their cattle, and they used stone in the Neolithic period and metal in the Bronze Age for their tools and weapons ... Undoubtedly as civilisation

---

26 Personal correspondence.

advanced and more land came under cultivation the fairy people must have mingled more and more with the settled population, till many of them entered the villages and became indistinguishable from the 'mortals'.[27]

They were indeed small in stature compared to the later invaders – probably no more than five feet tall at best; but they certainly did not live in buttercups or tulips! In fact, they lived in circular huts which were sunk into the ground to a depth of two or three feet. The roofs of these huts were supported by a central pole and wooden frame, the entire structure then covered in turf and bracken and shrubs, so that they looked like mounds, or small hills. These were the People of the Hills – the fairies and the witches. These are the descendants of those cave-dwellers who worshipped the Stag God in the Ariege, and who danced to the mystic tune of that God from Le Fourneau du Diable. Gwyn ap Nudd is his title on the British Isle, and we can give him the personal name of Herne. Merlin, Lailoken, Suibhne Gelt, and all the rest were his priests.

The fays – let us call them that – were not, however, some distant and doomed race that can mean no more to us than some Palaeolithic graffiti and a few myths. The fays no longer exist because they intermarried with those races that came afterward. The fays are to be found within our furthest ancestors. There is fay blood in all of us. They, and their pantheons – simple though they were – are part of our genetic structure. Soon, we will learn to meet up with them.

**The young lad writes with a certain confidence bordering on smugness, unaware of the insights to come. The faeries at the bottom of my garden have bothered me for some years but to be honest I can't say with confidence where the Elementals end, the Ancestors begin, or the bright spirits of the Sidhe power into my awareness. I think I must approach them now as I advised earlier with respect to the myriad deities and Recensions of Egypt and start with one small contact.**

**Beyond my garden, among the trees, I see the fays now as a race which exists parallel with ours. Sometimes they can step into our world,**

---

27 Margaret Murray, *The God of the Witches* (London: Oxford University Press, 1953), pp. 52-53

less frequently we can enter theirs. They have a hive mentality and lack our free will. Not all of them like us, because the worst of our society and industry is having damaging effects in their world.

The staggeringly psychic Canon Anthony Duncan, an exorcist for the Church of England, once yarned about a fay who emerged in his house after he had been moving furniture. The fay berated him, and pointed out that it was having a knock-on effect in his own home. In future, the good reverend had to negotiate with his visitor before he moved anything. It was all to do with patterns, apparently.

There is more to that last comment than meets our three eyes, however, as I shall explain.

Dion Fortune's take on one aspect of the faery beings was seen in her beautiful autobiography *Psychic Self Defence*:

> There are other forms of life as well as ours whose sphere of evolution impinges upon the earth. In the realm of folk-lore we constantly meet with the idea of intercourse between the human and fairy kingdoms; of the marriage of a human being with a fairy spouse...
>
> There are many of us who have met people who might well be described as non-human, soulless, in that the ordinary human motives are not operative with them, nor do the ordinary human feelings prompt or inhibit them. We cannot but love them, for they have great charm, but we cannot but dread them as well, for they spread an infinitude of suffering around them. Although seldom deliberately evil, they are singularly detrimental to all with whom they come into contact. They, for their part, are lonely and unhappy in our midst... Gratitude, compassion, good faith morality and common honesty are utterly foreign to their natures... They are not immoral however, but simply non-moral.

Listen, she is talking about a race of beings that was scorned, feared and often locked away from sight. She is talking about the beings who were branded in her day as Mongols, Imbeciles, Idiots and Simpletons, who later had their descriptions softened to the term Mentally Handicapped and are now – for the moment – described as people with Learning Disabilities.

When I was in my 20s I took a temporary job on the nursing side in the lovely but now defunct Rock Hall House in Combe Down, Bath, and became enchanted by the young residents therein. During the 30 years that followed I worked with every kind of disability and multi-disability – physical/emotional/mental – from gorgeous mites with Down's Syndrome, up to deaf adults with 'challenging behaviour', Aspergers or downright psychopathy, some of whom were also convicted murderers. I did these jobs not because I was kind, or caring, but (a) because I got trapped, like humans become trapped in faeryland, not aware of the time that passed and (b) I had to support my family, and circumstances seem to conspire against me getting back into the mainstream teaching jobs for which I was trained.

I saw many people whom I can only think were faery beings trapped in human form, not quite able to relate/communicate/understand. The more able ones, branded as being within the autistic spectrum, had the obsession with patterns that Anthony Duncan's fay noted. I think we all have some autistic (or faery) traits within ourselves if we are honest.

I can only say that these people, by and large, had more grace and more innate goodness than most of us will ever know.

Gwyn ap Nudd has two main associations which might seem trivial in themselves, but which can lead us into some extraordinarily vast areas for research. The first association is with Glastonbury Tor, and the second is with the Wild Hunt.

The Tor, which simply means 'hill', has a reputation in England for power and sanctity which other nationalities find hard to understand. It is regarded as the holiest place in the British Isles, and possibly the rest of the world as a whole – if its most ardent admirers are to be believed. This may or may not be true. Certainly there is a staggering accretion of legends connected with the Tor and the town which have gathered like moths to the light.

There are many who believe that under the waters of a spring and the slopes of the Tor, which is topped by a 14th-century church tower, Joseph of Arimathea buried what became known as the Holy Grail. They also believe that when, on a nearby hill, he thrust his thorn staff into the ground, it took root to produce the distinctive Glastonbury Winter-flowering thorn-tree.

Still further, they believe that he built a church of wattle and daub on the site where the ruins of the great abbey now stand and that there he made the first conversions to Christianity in Britain. It has long been an English conceit that Joseph, as a merchant who traded in tin, made regular trips to the mines in the nearby Mendip Hills and brought his nephew Jesus with him on at least one occasion.

If this was so, then, at the time when they made the voyage, the town itself would have been an island in the middle of marshes and lakes. A shallow sea would, at flood tides, lap its way some 20 miles inland to the very foot of the Tor itself.

In about 688 A.D., King Ine of Wessex gave Glastonbury a monastery which was regarded as the most beautiful in the land. A tomb can still be seen within the grounds which the monks claimed to have been that of Arthur, although some folk secretly whispered that it was that of Gwyn. Other legends have it that Arthur and his knights are sleeping below the Tor, like Osiris, waiting for the moment when they will be needed to 'save the land' once more.

Geoffrey Ashe, the formidable Arthurian scholar, makes a potent case for the Tor being the wondrous temple described by Roman historians as the principal focus for the mysteries in Britain. In fact, the whole area has been seen as ringed by a zodiac formed by the natural features of the land – the heavens brought down and sealed within the Earth.

So it is here, in a small and otherwise unremarkable town which specializes in sheepskin products and a livestock market that the supreme examples of the Pagan and Christian Mysteries co-exist and indeed thrive.

Glastonbury, in the hearts of many, is the true power-centre of Britain: like the grail/cauldron/crystal ball, all things can be found within it if you know how and when to look. It may be a small town in Somerset to the earthly eye, but, to the visionary, it is a gateway to Avalon.

Glastonbury again... this prompts me to put another rock in my Zen garden but one dedicated to Cley Hill – which can also be a gateway to Avalon, if that is what you are attuned toward.

Although I had lived within 10 miles of Cley Hill for a number of years it was Dolores Ashcroft-Nowicki who alerted me to its potency. We drove past it in my battered but beloved Citroen 2CV on the way to see Christine Hartley; as the menacing aspect of the hill loomed on our left she waved an arm out of the window and called out cheerily: *Hello boys!* For a nano-second, perhaps through a kind of psychic resonance, I saw that the hill was alive with ancient but ever-young souls. Years later, when I started the *Inner Guide to the Megaliths*, I was compelled to find out everything I could about the place.

To make the point now, Cley Hill is one of the least known and yet most potent of centres within Britain, whose energies are entirely tuned to what the Christians saw as the Devil, but who is more truly the old Horned God of the West. It was from here that I got my battle cry: 'Glastonbury is for Cissies!'

Local legends insist that Cley Hill is the home to the King of the Faeries. His name is still preserved as Bugley (hence the nearby Bugley Barton Farm), which is a variant of Bogle, Buggle, Bwcca, Pwcca, Pook or Puck – and from which we ultimately derive the term Bogey Man. Dr. Anne Ross points out in her book about the Druid Prince exhumed from the peat in the Midlands that large horned beasts such as rams are said to guard/haunt places where the Buggle is felt to exist. In fact local tradition has it that a golden ram is buried deep within the hill, which is said to be riddled with tunnels. However, this may well be an overlap from the Templar days, when that order owned property at the foot of Cley Hill, if not the hill itself. The adjoining village of Temple still contains a few of their wraiths connected with the church of St Mary the Virgin which is always locked, and whose odd glowering mood has a tendency to cling to me long afterwards, like cobwebs.

There are two barrows on the top which are linked to the Iron Age. The larger one, ripped open by Sir Richard Colt-Hoare, was found to contain three ears of un-decayed wheat, the smaller one the bones of a man. Thus the former contains the essence of a deity, the latter the remains of its priest.

Next to it on the eastern side is 'Little Cley Hill' as the locals call it. From ground level this looks no more than a gentle surge in the land but from the top of 'Big Cley Hill' the proportions are as clear and certain as those of man-made Silbury Hill.

It is designated by archaeologists simply as an Iron Age Hill-fort. The upper level was quite clearly fenced off from the lower, where the common folk mingled and lived, much as our upper levels of consciousness are often separated from those mundane ones we use to get through the day. But in essence I am certain it was a ritual centre, a college which is only now starting to make its curriculum available to us.

The eastern side of Cley Hill slopes down and away from its summit like a concave dish laid at a steep angle. After a very short distance the base blends towards Little Cley Hill where the major and public rites and games were all held. Standing on the low, rounded top of the latter, voices can be heard from people high up on the eastern slopes of the larger mass: disembodied snatches of conversations which float and burst like bubbles in seemingly precise locations in the air. It is a trick of nature caused by the wind, and the dish-like shape of the hill at that side, but it creates a whispering gallery without walls, and a wondrous tool for the Sibyl in the light of the moon, the stillness of the dusk. And near that Moon Place too, on another slope, is what might be termed the Old Lady's House, the astral shell of a hut in the woods where women worked their own magic at the time of their menstruation, and from which storms can be summoned.

Not far away is the almost-forgotten Periwinkle Pond, called after one of the Fairy Court, and linked both with Fairy Oak and various sacrificial rites. Sometimes, when by a leap of consciousness the whole area is glimpsed in its primal essence, with almost hallucinogenic intensity, the bright spirits of the sidhe, the Faeries, are everywhere. And there are always cattle in the scene, somehow.

According to tradition there is a Gate atop of Glastonbury Tor which leads to the Otherworld/Underworld. It is here that Gwyn can be found and here that we can find our ways back to the thesis of the first chapter. Here the Horned God can be found guarding the Moon Gate behind which lie dragons, dead souls and the infinite sources of life itself. We are back to the concept of Osiris dwelling in the Tuat, but coming to the Gate at daily intervals to offer us entry. These are the Gods of Life and also of Death, as these qualities are seen as different sides of the same door.

### the caves and forests

It has always been argued by the occultist that peoples of previous ages, such as the fays, had faculties that have since atrophied in modern humanity. It is implied that the loss of these faculties was something of a minor Fall from a more blessed state. But that was not quite the case. These faculties certainly existed – and exist today. They can awaken with surprising ease when people find themselves living in isolated places for long periods of time. Silence shows that it has sensual, living qualities of its own, and that it is far more than simply an absence of noise. Isolation proves to be anything but seclusion. Those faculties that we imagined had been lost to the aeons come creeping out like timid mice. The Two Sights, and similar faculties, begin to open once more.

But, as Julian Jaynes has shown in his book, *The Origin of Consciousness in the Breakdown of the Bicameral Mind*, this can be seen more accurately as a description of the way humanity's mode of thinking changed from being right-brain dominated to find itself functioning essentially through the left hemisphere.

In crude and simple terms (the best kind there are), the left brain deals with intellect, analysis, linear thinking, cause-and-effect, mechanical time – all qualities that we can conveniently describe as Solar, and which relate to the Qabalistic sphere of Chokmah.

In contrast, the right brain is concerned with intuition, gestalt, non-linear thinking, synchronicity, and timelessness, which we might regard as being Lunar, and linked with the sphere of Binah.

As Jaynes asserts, from a non-occult viewpoint, tribal members would feel themselves to be part of a common consciousness. They would be aware of the presence of the departed and would be able to function collectively, as certain groupings within the animal and bird world so obviously do. The voice of their con-scienses would resonate in their mental ears with the voices of their dead fathers, or dead kings. Best of all, their dead kings.

> Osiris ... was the hallucinated voice of a dead king whose admonitions could still carry weight. And since he could still be heard [via right-brain consciousness], there is no paradox in the fact that the body from which the voice came should be mummified, with all the equipment of the tomb providing life's necessities ... There was no mysterious power that emanated from him; simply his remembered voice which appeared in

hallucination to those who had known him and which could admonish or suggest even as it had before he stopped moving and breathing?[28]

The principle is correct, no doubt about it. Jaynes, however, does not take into account the possibility that such inner voices, heard via the right-brain functions, could often be exactly what they seem. In any case the whole scheme must be counterbalanced by those researchers who turn the flow of consciousness around 90 degrees, in a sense, and attribute these same qualities to the functions of the cerebrum and cerebellum instead.

It is interesting to note that when the occultist Dion Fortune described the consciousness of the Atlantean commoner, she noted, rather disparagingly, that they had little more intelligence than dogs. Today, she might well ascribe those dog-like characteristics to the tight, tribal collective of right-brain consciousness, as seen from afar by a 20th century visionary.

The point is that with this right-brain consciousness, there was an absolute certainty that man did survive after death. However they expressed this survival in their religious systems, death, as an experience, was completely devoid of the terrors that it has for us today. It was not a matter of faith. It is not a matter of holding up some desperately-held belief system as a shield against the nightmare ... the reality of the Otherworld and each person's survival therein was part of everyday experience.

The Gods of the Old Religions, if we may call them that, contained within themselves Life and Death, Light and Darkness, Giving and Taking, Male and Female, Outer and Inner. They balanced; they were one. There was no exaltation of one at the expense of the other. So must the Tor balance the Abbey, the Pagan with the Christian, the hill with the valley.

Taking up a crude but immediate analogy: society today is rather like a branch plucked from a tree, split part of the way down its length and pulled apart. The tensions at the end of the split, where the whole branch begins, are enormous. As the outward pressure on the split prongs continues, disaster becomes imminent. The branch is likely to burst apart entirely. Society, shaped liked the divining rods used

---

28 Julian Jaynes, *The Origin of Consciousness in the Breakdown of the Bicameral Mind.* (Boston: Houghton Mifflin Co., 1976), p. 187.

by the old-fashioned dowsers, quivers before our astonished gaze. So the pressure must be relaxed, the split healed, Life and Death seen to channel the same saps, and the branch placed carefully into the earth in the hope that it might flower once again.

I used to think in terms of the Old Religion as if it were a universal, matriarchal system, although I wasn't alone in that respect. Now, I see that I was unintentionally closer to a truth when I thought of it in the plural as I did in that isolated sentence above – Old Religions: people across the world doing their own things in opposition to established systems, following inner-world patterns and scripts perhaps, but by no means united by any dogma. Perhaps, now, we might just use the term: Western Mystery Tradition, which is a broad enough church for everyone.

Bill Gray once said that he had known of many attempts in the occult/magical movements to create a united front but that none of them had worked. The best that he expected of his own 'Sangreal Sodality' was that separate individuals across the world would quietly form their own little groups and search for Light in their own ways.

The Glastonbury region is an image of the universe, and therefore of Humanity. We can find anything we want there – Holy Grails, saints, Once and Future Kings, mystic caverns, ley-lines. But we have to find them in ourselves first. We are all Isles of Glass set within shallow seas. "Behind the smiling mirror, and Behind the smiling moon, Follow, Follow …" as T. S. Eliot said.

Balance is needed. Between the hemispheres of the brain, the left and the right, the outward and inward. Gwyn ap Nudd is one of those gods who can show us precisely where the dividing line is, and how to make use of it. What he does not want – not these days – is our worship. We need the gods and the gods need us. We need the gods to teach us things; they need us to experience. The flow is entirely mutual and two-way.

This is neither heresy, hubris, nor megalomania, but a way forward into a New Age. The old initiatic cry: "There is no part of me which is not also part of the Gods!" can now be inverted to read: "There is no part of the Gods which can not be found in me." So Gwyn can be as easily contacted by means of a solitary lighted candle in a small apartment in the heart of an American city as he can upon the windswept heights of Glastonbury Tor. It all has to do with heart, and with intention.

Ultimately, we will show how Gwyn is concerned with both the spirit of place and the place of spirit, and deal with the concept of the land as a living, knowing entity. Neither of them want our worship, but they do want our work. The Earth in particular is a battered, abused and raped woman. Such a woman does not want to be worshipped – she wants help, healing, and understanding. The time for crude worship is past.

So Gwyn rises to us in dreams and visions. He can bring us those salves and unguents which can help heal the bruises and breaks within the world and within ourselves. We could do worse than become his priests and priestesses for a while, knowing that one day we will ride at his back, with the Wild Hunt – when our own earthly cares have been left far behind.

The Wild Hunt, whether galloping from Glastonbury Tor or any number of other sites, is one of those themes which has left its mark in European folklore without anyone being particularly clear as to its true nature. At one time, it was seen in the skies as often as UFOs are today, and it provoked the same kind of excitement and awe. Its first recorded appearance in England was at Peterborough in Lincolnshire in the year 1127:

> these hunters were black, and huge and ugly, and they rode on black horses and deer. They were seen in the very deer-park of the town of Peterborough ... and the monks heard the blasts of the horns which they blew in the night.[29]

These Hunts, sometimes in the sky and sometimes through the forest rides, were seen all over Europe. In the German tradition, it is a spectral hunter with a pack of dogs, particularly associated with the Black Forest. In France, *Le Grand Veneur* courses through Fontainebleau Forest; in Britain, the honours are shared between Herne, of Windsor Forest, and Gwyn himself; while it is Odin, or Woden, who leads

---

29 The Anglo-Saxon Chronicle, quoted by Tolstoy, *op. cit.*

the spectral company through more northerly climes. In some cases, the huntsmen themselves were held to be the souls of pagan corpses, forever condemned to pursue a mystic hart across the darkling worlds. In others, they were the souls of dead warriors.

There is something almost touching about the former: a vision, perhaps, of medieval man's conscience allowing him a mystic glimpse of those lost parts of himself coursing through the stars in pursuit of a rapidly vanishing god – the true god of the land of his heart, if he were to face it.

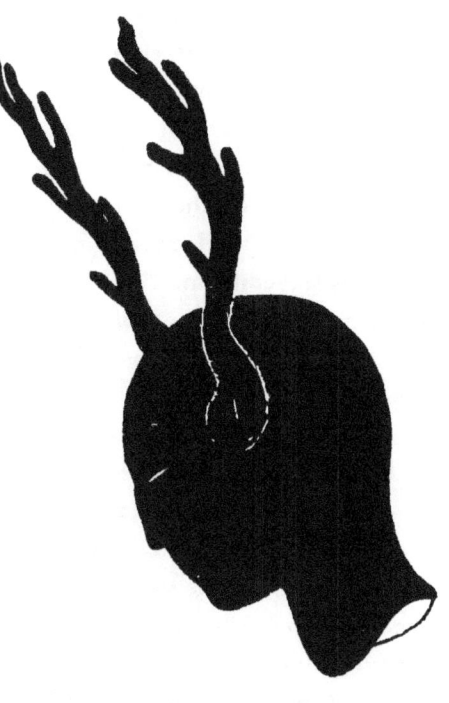

So it was Herne, from his home in the royal forest of Windsor, who led the Hunt among the English in later centuries, while the Celts, with their older subconscious memories, referred to him as Gwyn ap Nudd, and taught that he gathered up dead souls and carried them to his realm via that Gate within the Hill of Vision, or Glastonbury Tor. If he was ever seen accompanied by his Hounds of Hell, like the bean-sidhe (banshees) of Irish myth, it was a sure sign that mortals witnessing the vision were themselves about to die. In time, in more ways than one, people did not look at all. In time, in more ways than one, people were no longer able to see.

Several modern magicians have had the experience of being denied access to the Tor – and other holy hills – as if by an inner command. A command which they knew they must not, could not, deny. In each case the reason, if that is the appropriate term, was that the 'Hosting of the Sidhe' was in progress at the summit. This is a comparatively benign but no less potent version of the Wild Hunt, as the Sidhe (shee) are the faery race of Ireland. We have also already mentioned those mysterious conglomerations of lights frequently seen today emanating from and returning back into such places.

Sometimes the old souls and perhaps lost souls gather at the edge of my garden; I wonder what they want. They rarely tell me, even in obscure ways. Reading about the Wild Hunt and the Hosting of the Sidhe I am reminded of the many times when Cley Hill has called me in a way that I could not resist and somehow made my complicated life suddenly and miraculously clear enough for me to visit. Sometimes it entered my dreams, or slid in between them and my waking consciousness, so that I found myself there – in some sense – in spirit, and bewildered by it all.

Once, after just such impulses, I spent a morning on the summit, summoning up all the souls who had become earthbound on the top of the hill, almost a leader of my own Wild Hunt. And so I found myself on a grey November morning leading a procession of these earthbound wretches down to the Moon Place, with the injunction being that I must not look back. It was a festival, a delight, I could sense them all behind me – a few dozen perhaps – and hear the babble of a happy crowd, a strangely young crowd, eager to go on a journey. When I got to the sacred place and opened the Gates, it was as though they soared upward, rushing, but with thanks.

On another time, circling the large barrow widdershins and invoking Bugley himself by the simplest of means, the crust of the hill seemed to become wafer thin. I had the feeling of being on top of a huge, green crystal hollowness that could at any moment shatter under my weight. And if I didn't see Bugley himself I at least glimpsed his realm, and the green/gold, other dimensional light of Inner Earth.

All these things I can see within the Zen Garden today, via the two white rocks representing Big and Little Cley Hill.

Frequently, all of these have been lumped together under the heading of UFO phenomena. While it would be ridiculous to reject entirely the notion that we are being visited from the stars, the truth about many of these lights is more closely related to the 'aliveness' of certain places within the landscape. It is particularly hills that come alive in discernible ways.[30]

---

[30] For reasons now forgotten I was using a bull-roarer late one night atop of Westbury White Horse. I wanted to see if I could summon spirits. Instead my wife Margaret and I saw a vast UFO behind clouds. I wanted to be beamed up: she wanted us to flee. She drove, we fled. I still think I missed a chance.

### ••• the caves and forests •••

Watching these emanations from the hill of your choice is like watching neurons firing in the brain. It is the consciousness of the hill that we see in dynamic action. Because we become linked to this particular hill in a magical relationship, we are also watching our own neurons firing. In a way, these apparently intelligent lights *are* from beyond this world. They are from the most distant future and the remotest past, for they are expressions of our most ancient genetic consciousness.

All this will be discussed again in due course, but we must get back to the inevitable question: "What is being pursued by the Hunt?" In that first recorded vision from Peterborough the answer is already clear: a wounded hart. But although there is also, often, the confident answer 'dead souls,' in too many of the other sightings the spectral horsemen are involved in more of a Wild Ride, a frenzied gallop behind their leader. Can this have any relevance to us here and now, with all our modern concerns?

A partial answer can be found in Mediterranean sources. For example, this can be seen in the story of Actaeon, who happened to see the Goddess Artemis (known as Diana to the Romans) bathing naked. Artemis, who possessed a magical silver bow, hunted Actaeon down with her hounds, transformed him into a stag, and killed him with her bow. According to Robert Graves (*The White Goddess*), Actaeon was: '... a sacred king of the pre-Hellenic stag cult, torn to pieces at the end of his reign of 50 months.'

We might speculate from this that the horned figure who leads the Hunt across the lightning-flecked sky is himself the object of pursuit in an echo of the Cult of the Sacred King. The hunter, as the saying goes, becomes the hunted. So there is Actaeon, turned into a stag and torn to pieces. There is Osiris, the Horned God, torn to pieces by Set and his many animal-like companions. And there is an oblique cross-linking between Osiris and the Hunter through the association of the Egyptian god with the constellation of Orion. The latter was a giant hunter, noted for his beauty, who was blinded by Oenopian,[31] and finally slain by Diana (known as Artemis to the Greeks).

We can indeed witness this Wild Hunt on many levels, both magical and mundane, and one as important as the other. The Hunt

---

31 Orion assaulted King Oenopian's daughter. Personally, as the father of four girls, I think Orion got off lightly.

is integral to atmospheric disturbances – storm, lightning, and high wind – with the spectral company part and parcel of the turbulence.

It is said that such storms often accompany great souls entering or leaving the world. This is especially true when the soul concerned – consciously or otherwise – was or is about to be linked with the land in some shamanic sense.

Anyone who rises to any prominence, in any profession or group, invariably becomes aware of the hounds and jackals that slowly start to gather behind him. Among modern celebrities, particularly Anglo-American political figures, this is especially noticeable.

It is a curious comment upon, and perhaps indictment of, our times that whereas ancient kings and leaders had to prove their fitness for office by virtue of virility and fertility, nowadays the dogs of the media sniff over their trails for the slightest sign of sexual transgression. The French, who at least in this area have wisdom, can never understand why British and American politicians feel honour-bound to resign – or are hounded into resigning – whenever they are caught in some sexual transgression, often from the remote past. But this was always going to be an end result of the 'sterility cult' created by dominant aspects of the Christian church.

Sexual naughtiness among celebrities apart, aspects of this experience are fundamental to the workaday world, too. The more we attain as individuals, the more our inner fertilities find singular expressions that can push us out beyond the pack, the more likely it becomes that the pack will want to rip us apart. This is not paranoia, or shouldn't be. It is more simply a knowledge that we live out rituals in our lives which, however crude and corrupted they are, still can link us with energies from the oldest times.

All of this takes us back to that Moon Gate which lies between the Human and the Natural Worlds, and is guarded by that Horned God who is part man, part beast, and who can show us the way to the oldest parts of ourselves. If, in the historical sense, his worship became as dismembered as he regularly was, then we can find it echoed today within Spiritualist and Wiccan circles.

At first glance, this seems absurd, but they are in fact two parts of one formidable equation. Many spiritualists today are linked by previous existences in which they functioned, quite simply, as witches. Unfortunately, the spiritualist movement itself is too often limited by

## the caves and forests

its rather brittle and apparently shallow dogma, and shaded over by the infernally Christian nature of its approach. It is invariably (and unfairly) seen as the refuge of the weak, simple, and elderly. On the other hand, as far as Wicca goes, there are very few witches around today who have one tenth of the extraordinary talents and healing abilities the best spiritualist mediums have. They know a great deal about occult philosophies, and have entirely laudable 'green' attitudes, but they are too often sadly lacking in any power.

If the two were able to combine, somehow, so that we could get a spiritualist movement with passionate Nature links (in the magical sense), and which was not afraid of sex, or else a witch with the full and deep complement of spiritualist powers, then we would have a potent mix indeed. We would have a shamanic figure ripe to wear the crown of a near-forgotten god.

In a sense, both Spiritualism and Witchcraft today lie scattered at either side of the Moon Gate as fragments of a once cohesive power. They are the broken halves of a crown – the crown itself being a stylised version of the stag's helm or similar ritual adornment. Someday this crown will be retrieved and restored.

An American woman will appear who will be a child of Coyote (who is really Anubis letting his hair down, so to speak). She will have a vision of a bear, an open mouth, an expanse of cold, dark water, and a place of glittering sharpness. In time, she will join these two traditions together and take us all a little further through that Gate.

**I don't know where I got that from. Though several readers did contact me claiming the vision as referring to themselves.**

Apart from the Horned God pure and simple, there are other figures from history and legend who have become imbued with that green light that shines from within him. Any figure with strong Earth or Water connections is ripe for investiture as a priest of the Horned God.

Robin Hood is the classic example. In fact, the name Robin

(meaning 'Bright Flame') was often ascribed to the god of those witches who came up against their Christian inquisitors. Witches in Somerset claimed that their god was called up simply by calling the name Robin three times. A simple enough method, but one which is entirely effective today, as we shall see.

Robin of the Hood may well be a reference to those helmets which the priests wore, and which were necessarily large enough to support the horns of whatever deity they used. Or it may be that, with the great linguistic changes that occurred in this medieval period, the term Robin of the Wood became pronounced Robin 'Ood – which still later linguistic changes rationalised and modernised as Robin Hood. (In England, the stress is on the third syllable of the name rather than on the first, as in the American pronunciation.) Robin of the Hood and/or Robin of the Wood would be the local deity whose energies were mediated by the appropriate priest and priestess.

Of course, the name 'Bright Flame' is one that can make sparks fly within the imagination of any romantically inclined magician – the bright flame, the Light from Darkness, the shining spirit of the woods. There are links, too, between Robin Hood/Wood and

*Robin Goodfellow, c.1628*

··· the caves and forests ···

the intriguing figure of Robin Goodfellow, the guiding spirit of more than one coven, who was described as a powerful, horned and bearded man, yet one who was pure and virile goat from the waist down – even to the cloven hooves. He carried a witches broom over one shoulder, a wooden phallus of sorts in his right hand, and had a hunting horn slung over his other shoulder. He was an early 17th century answer to the Great God Pan, as far as some contemporary academics were concerned, but they were always missing the real truth about him.

Nevertheless Pan, Cheiron, the Aker and all those many entities from Mediterranean myth systems which are part human and part beast can be found at the same place within our consciousness as Gwyn, waiting in that timeless manner of theirs for us to make the necessary links.

Of course, it was easier to make these links in previous ages, for reasons already given. Then, communities were isolated in ways and to degrees that we cannot easily appreciate today. Each community had its own family of invisible creatures that bonded with them, and with whom they worked on outer and inner levels. There was indeed a complete unity between these levels. There was no difference. But the onus of accurate and detailed communication was laid at the door of that shamanic figure who later came to be described as a witch. The ability to work in this way came to be something of a family trait. Peculiar talents were passed on through the genes from one generation to another, kept within the ranks of specific families, and this only began to diminish when the communities themselves began to be fragmented by the changing times.

**I absorbed all of that from William G. Gray, expounding on this theme as he pumped away at the strange paraffin heating device he used in his downstairs study while his wife Bobbie leaned on the doorway, smoking and nodding. I was always somewhat scared of Bill, though he never showed me anything other than kindness; I quite adored Bobbie. Looking back, and looking beyond my garden wall, I don't think either of them ever mentioned the word 'faery' to me. Still, that race would have been lost on me then. I did prick up my ears intensely when he started talking about Mars and the cataclysm which destroyed the civilisations**

there, but he got side-tracked somehow, and ended up telling me what a shit Dennis Wheatley was instead.

In an oblique reference to these communities there is an extraordinary piece of folk-memory preserved in John Michell's *Megalithomania*:

> [At Callanish on the Isle of Lewis] the old people still held certain families in special respect and esteem as 'belonging to the Stones' ... The old man also told him that when the sun rose on Midsummer morning 'Something' came to the Stones, walking down the great avenue heralded by the cuckoo's call. He had described the 'Something' by a word [which] was probably pre-Gaelic, and from a root common to the British group of languages. It meant, they thought, the Shining, or Pure, or White one ... and had probably been the epithet of a god.[32]

These are the People of the Stones who are just as involved with the 'Bright Flame' as the People of the Wood, or Hood. In both cases they know that the land is alive, and that the spirit(s) behind their own localised portion of it had an interest in working with them, and for them, if they could just understand the spirit properly.

In another Element, too, there is the figure of Sir Francis Drake, whom the Spaniards called El Draco, or the Dragon – which is what his name actually means. An extraordinary man who explored vast areas of a hitherto unsuspected world, he became widely regarded after his death as having been larger than life. He is thought to have had definite magical powers, and his drum is said to beat even today when England is in peril. Many people through the centuries have claimed to have heard this beat, which might be likened to the heart beat of the nation itself. His former manor, Combe Sydenham in Devon, resonates with some peculiar energies. But best of all, as a proof of identity, local legends after his death coincidentally described him as the foremost rider in the Wild Hunt.

---

32 John Michell, *Megalithomania*. (London: Thames and Hudson, 1982), pp. 102-103.
   I am certain the word in question was *gwen* or a variant.

··· the caves and forests ···

Robin of the Wood claimed the Earth and the trees for his domain; Sir Francis Drake had the Sea and its waves. Under the masks, both men were the same.

Any hero figure closely associated with the Elements can be used to crack open the Moon Gate even if these figures (a) never existed or (b) existed, but in reality had no interest in any spiritual matters. Frontiersmen provide a fine example for the American magician – men who lived on the edge of Nature and who attracted tales and taller tales about their deeds ... Daniel Boone, Davy Crockett, Kit Carson – they can all be used. Or rather, their images can be used, which is not quite the same thing. If obscure Chancellors[33] from obscure periods in British history can be used by the followers of Dion Fortune to bring through material and experience of unquestionable value, and if the witches' contacts with Robin of the Wood can do similar, then there is nothing absurd about expecting that one day the King of the Wild Frontier might come to do the same for his own people.

In literary terms, we also have the reality of the Gypsy and the image of the gamekeeper to provide us with some further lore. Some believe the Gypsies to be remnants of a ''gyptian' tribe which made the great migration from their homeland along the Nile, bearing arcane knowledge with them. Whether Gypsies are decayed Egyptian stock, or an Indic people speaking the Indo-European language of Romany, or remnants of the fays – or all three – they are people who live outside society, closer to Nature than the rest of us. They are generally credited with hereditary faculties such as the Two Sights, which often made them objects of fear. On another continent entirely, the Native Indians have exactly the same role and position, although they seem to have retained their Mysteries in a far more cohesive and enduring manner. Indeed, it can be argued that they, more than any other racial group, contain the secrets of the next Age.

So, clearly, the Moon Gate is a crowded place. Or it would be, rather, if we continued to look at it with a universal eye. Soon, we will learn to take a gentle flail to all these images – for at the moment that is all they are, empty images – and drive away all that do not concern us, flicking at them as Pharaoh must once have flicked at the desert flies. Once that is done, we will be left with our two originals, the

---

33 Lords Eldon, Erskine and Thomas More were primary inner contacts within the Fraternity of the Inner Light.

Horned God and the Horned Goddess, however we choose to name them. We will learn to pick up their messages at whatever frequencies they broadcast upon.

But before we can do that we must tie up some loose ends, and bring the main themes of the book full circle. We must look at the Cult of the Sacred Kings and the Sacrificed Gods, and learn how even in these obscure realities from the darkest ages of world history, a message for the brightest futures can still be found.

# And the Places of Sacrifice

In the realm of the Celts there were four great occasions when the veil between the worlds was thinner than usual, and when it became easier to pass through. These were on the feast-days of: Candlemas, February 2nd; Beltaine, May 1st; Lammas, August 1st; Samhain, November 1st. In truth, however, the actual calendrical date was far less important than the night of the nearest full moon.

Of all the occasions, Samhain was in many ways the most striking. This was the beginning of the Blotmonath, the Bloodmonth, when the cattle and other livestock (known as quick-goods) were slaughtered and preserved to last the communities throughout the incoming winter. Samhain was also when the ancestors, the honourable spirits of the dead, were prone to gather in a yearly communion of loved ones, both living or long since gone.

It was in these months that Kings were sacrificed, or ritually slain. Specifically, it was in the Bloodmonth that Camelot came to an end, when a bright young King shed his blood upon the land to release the best of impulses in those people who adored him.

Once, in a life far beyond this one, I received the news of that death while still in the body of a boy fretting on the edge of puberty, within a cold and windswept world. It is the clearest of all my 'far memories' in many ways. I was looking over a scrubbed wooden counter on which stood some brightly coloured jars and bottles, just tall enough to rest my chin on the ridges of the wood made smooth by the countless hands and elbows which rested upon it. There was the smell of cooking in some primitive apparatus; the smell of the grease and the fat which attended the art. A stink of smoke was on everyone's clothes, and a portly woman with a dark blue apron was saying in a guttural voice:

'Aye, he's deed ... Ah'm tellin' ye he's deed!' The voices around, on my side of the counter, muttered disbelief, the faces bearing a kind of exultant sorrow at hearing such staggering news. *Ner, Ner,* I thought. *Nivver! Nivver in this weorld...*

But this is not, in the reincarnational sense, a past life that I am recalling, but the purest memory of having been in Allington's fish and chip shop, in my home town in the north-east of England, as I heard from the astonished lady with the battered cod the astonishing news that President Kennedy had been assassinated. It was a death whose reverberations spread across the world and rippled through us all, one of those moments that no-one ever forgets. That, after all, is what the death of Sacred Kings is all about.

Now, absurd as it may seem at first, Kennedy, whose name means 'The Helmeted Chief,' can be seen as another in the long line of Sacred Kings, even if the patterns of his 'kingship' had become distorted. There was his ability to talk easily to and identify with the common man, even if his own family were far removed from their level in terms of wealth and status. There was the family itself, perceived as being both charmed and cursed, as 'special' families inevitably are. There was his extraordinary sexual appetite, which was like a wry interpretation of the Fertility God's true function.

There was that seductive and indefinable aura of his which was only exceeded by that of his wife Jackie. She was, if not a 'white shadow' in the true sense of the term, at least a gleaming aspect of his presidency in other ways.[34] There was even the name 'Camelot,' bestowed upon his administration by the media because of the innate glitter that seemed to shine from within. And there was the death itself, before the eyes of the world, which had been foretold, warned against, and indeed fully expected among some pundits.

There were also the staggering parallels with Lincoln's death, which prompted some to drag up karmic theories. And then there was the springing-up of the mysteries – the conspiracy theories, the cover-ups – all the rough and muffled echoes of those mysteries which must surround the death of any Sacrificial King.

And *then* there came the spate of rumours about his after-death state (these most significant of all), which insisted that Kennedy was

---

34 Oddly enough her maiden name Bouvier can mean either herdsman, or 'resembling an ox'.

not dead but paralysed, and that at some time – some future moment of national peril – their 'Helmeted Chief' would be wheeled out to inspire America with hope and courage anew.

All this may seem absurd or impossible. Yet, on some levels, it is infinitely true.

Kennedy was by no means the only American hero to fit into these parameters. Walt Disney's body was supposedly preserved in cryogenic tanks (like Merlin in his crystal cave) until the era when science could revive him. Jim Morrison of the Doors rock group was never really buried in Paris but is in fact living in pleasant obscurity somewhere in Europe; while Elvis Presley is not only alive but is regularly witnessed in unlikely locations throughout the Western world – a true case of the King being dead, but no one allowing him to die.

Yet all of this is not to suggest that President Kennedy or anyone else of his kind was part of an occult/political system which ensured a ritual murder according to a primordial pattern. What I am suggesting is that there exists within our consciousness a matrix akin to that found within solutions of copper sulphate, which causes crystals to take shape in the same general form every time. These matrices, or inner structures, are as old as time – and in fact time is the agent which is instrumental to their formation.

The myth and lesson of the Sacred King is fundamental to Western consciousness in one way or another and finds expressions in the most unexpected but clearly recognisable ways. John F. Kennedy had to be assassinated, for the death of a sex god, like that of a sex goddess, should always be extraordinary. It is the least we can demand. Slow decay is not for them, nor increasing decrepitude, so that generations come along to wonder what we ever saw in them. It is the sudden exit at the height of their erotic power which makes us remember and even revere. Fans of Marilyn Monroe, with whom he was connected, will appreciate that.

**I adore Conspiracy Theories. I could sit here on the edge of my garden wall all day, reading nothing else. I accept almost all of them, though I do not believe the Moon landings were faked. I had such fun writing *Dark Light*, which is both a dig at the whole genre but also an appreciation. I hope I live long enough to learn the truth about the**

murders of John Paul I, President Kennedy, Marilyn Monroe, Princess Diana and Dr. David Kelly. And I ache to find out the unvarnished truth behind Roswell, Cydonia, Rendlesham Forest and whether the Duke of Edinburgh really was a giant baby-eating lizard.

To understand this fully, we must now begin to look at something of the history behind it all, and learn that there are ancient sources of energy behind each and every individual. These energy sources can be drawn upon as needed – and they sometimes radiate into our lives whether we are aware of them or not.

In ancient days the King was divine. The King was God – or God's representative on Earth. And the King was also of the people. In prehistoric Britain, there were as many kings as there were tribes. They reigned in their multitudes over a multitude of kingdoms. During the time of their reign, each King was protected and cosseted by his people. Nothing was too much trouble. So if the King wished for something within the possibilities of their simple world, it was granted him.

In many and strange ways they worshipped their own particular King; and then, at the specified end of his reign, they slew him, and spilled his blood upon the ground in order to revitalise it, tore his body apart (perhaps even ate some of it), and then invested his eager successor with whatever trappings of regency they possessed.

Romulus, the legendary founder of Rome, was said to have been cut to pieces by the patricians, who carried the pieces away under their robes and buried them in the earth. A similar custom was practised in early Scandinavia: King Halfdan the black was drowned in the spring when the ice was breaking and his body was divided into three pieces, one piece being buried in each of the three provinces of his kingdom.[35]

Once again the Osirian matrix-machine has been set on replay.

Even the passionate urge to remove the internal organs from the Sacrificed King is a direct echo of the Egyptians' removal and storage of internal organs in the mummification process. If an individual,

---

35 Margaret Murray, *The Divine King in England*. (London: Faber, 1964), p. 28.

community, or province could share in the substance of the King, they would necessarily come to express his innate fertility also.

In the earliest of European cultures this inner aspect of kingship – which may or may not have derived from an Osirian original – was to be perpetuated for immense periods of time.

There are hints also that in some earlier cultures, the actual powers of kingship were portioned between two figures, whom we might term the Bright and Dark Twins[36] – which echoes certain concepts connected with the magic of Sirius. The Bright Twin had all the regal powers, all the outward authority that we traditionally associate with the crown; but he was balanced and supported at all times by the Dark Twin, the shaman figure who expresses the inward side of the tribal mind and who, more than anyone else, maintains and clarifies the links with the ancestors and guiding spirits. In a sense, they were akin to the left and right sides of the brain, together helping the tribal consciousness function as a single unit.

The sacrifice was made at the end of a specific period of time, in accordance with certain stellar configurations. It was almost unheard of for the victim to refuse to be sacrificed. In any case, death in those days was no more than a door through which the soul entered the innermost Mysteries of the Earth; and so the victim was soon able to peep back out at his tribe again from the other side.

It was the Dark Twin who did the slaying, he who guided the Bright King's spirit through its passing. In later years, in societies that were very different, and under kingships which were more truly national in scope, the Dark Twin became the Divine Substitute. In order to preserve the (successful) King's term, the Dark Twin offered his life in exchange. This, we might presume, was the real origin of a concept and practice that later degenerated into the medieval use of 'whipping boys' who received those punishments more properly due to young princes to whom they were bound from birth.

**How 'true' is all this? Re-reading it now I can tell you with confidence that it is as true as my Zen garden, as true as the Atlantean stories behind Dion Fortune's *Sea Priestess*. That is to say while it has a certain**

---

36 One of the finest magical novels ever written, up there with the *The Sea Priestess* and *Moon Magic*, is Marion Campbell's *Dark Twin*. She got her inspiration from Robert Graves and her own inner sources.

reality and impact on inner and imaginal levels there is – probably – no historical substance at all.

These are notions derived from the scholarship (however wayward), intuitions (however flaky), and speculations (admirably fervent) of obvious culprits such as Robert Graves, Margaret Murray, Michael Harrison and others. In the 1980s and 90s, all sorts of gates were being opened and a whole mass of pagan types injured themselves and others leaping through them toward this new-ancient landscape beyond, each claiming to have worked magic as members of traditions which – they insisted – had existed for generations.

A folk-belief from Brittany springs to my mind of the Ankou, a kind of pagan Angel of Death who travels about the country in a large, black coach pulled by four black horses, accompanied by two ghostly figures on foot. At night it is heard creaking along the road. It halts at a door, gathers up another soul and moves on.

I think we all piled onto a kind of band-wagon or ankou-wagon in those days looking for a new kind of life and light. The ideas seemed right at the time; so much of them seem to be regarded today as fact. While I still accept the notion of the Sacred King, I now wonder whether the whole adjunct of the Dark Twin seems now to be too poetic, too seamless.

Perhaps it is a case of creating a past to make a perfect future for ourselves. Or creating a pseudo-historical tableau (is that the right word?) which might help us make sense of powerful but unseen impulses.

I suppose that if, as the highly respected and accepted Quantum Professors tell us, everything that can happen does happen, it might well be the case that everything that might have happened did happen. Thus a world of Dark and Bright Twins somehow did run parallel to ours, like one of the grooves raked in my garden by the tines, and just as real in its own time/space/event line.

Bizarrely, I believe that I did bump into a parallel self once, at the gates of King Alfred's College in Winchester. When I was 17 I became obsessed with going to this teacher-training college even though I knew nothing about Winchester, nor could have pointed it out on a map. I day-dreamed about the place intensely, but equally intense family circumstances stopped me applying and so I went to nearby Newcastle instead.

### ··· and the places of sacrifice ···

Many years later when I visited Christine Hartley in Winchester Hospital, I wandered out the back and was startled – astounded is the right word – to find myself at the very gates of the college. For a moment I felt as though I were in a pulsating stream of energy and imagery, as if all the possibilities, personalities and events of the life I would have experienced had I gone there were coursing through me. This was not a case of the poignant, gentle *But ... What If?* that I had experienced with respect to Normandi Ellis. This was visceral, more like having my hands clenched on an electrified fence as I tried to go over to somewhere that I shouldn't. Anyone watching might have thought I was doing a kind of St. Vitus Dance because I was drunk. But a whole Other Life which had run parallel to my own seemed to criss-cross inside me, like a piece of Celtic knot-work.

So – who knows? – perhaps we can view all of Margaret Murray's speculations as absolutely true – though not necessarily in this life stream. We can certainly get them to work for us.

In later eras (and we are talking in terms of millennia now), it was felt that the King had to die not only as a means of ensuring continued fertility, but as a means of cleansing the people of evil.

There was a dim reflection of this in the last century, an old folk-memory which asserted that the way to avoid disease in a herd of cattle was to single out one cow and slaughter it in a ritually appropriate manner. Whatever portions of bad luck were due to the herd or its owner would thus be confined to just one clearly identified beast, so the rest would be left alone. We find continuing echoes of this in our own lives, too, when some poor wretch in our neighbourhood falls prey to some disaster in the form of illness or accident. Underneath the concern, underneath the compassion, hidden away behind a natural desire to help the person or their family in any way we can, there is also a very deep and ancient hope that malignancy, like some ravening beast, has chosen its prey – your own family can survive for another year at least.

In purely psychological terms, the Divine King made extraordinary sense. No one could, or would, begrudge the wealth and trappings of regal power knowing that whatever rancour might develop, whatever hates or jealousies or grievances might arise, all would be redressed at the moment of sacrifice when the King, as a man, would get his 'comeuppance.' We can tolerate a lot from our leaders if we can be assured of that.

This is, of course, the question of Nature being balanced, of things being put to rights, and justice being done. It is Maat in action. Problems only arose when a King proved particularly good and well-loved, and no truly adequate successors could be found at the end of the reign, which usually lasted seven years. In an ideally functioning world, that successor would himself be 'of the blood' – perhaps not necessarily as a direct offspring, but certainly possessing that peculiar spark which gave the Divine King his singular radiance.

It was the furtherance of this spark, this genetic heritage, which caused the pharaohs to sleep with their sisters. This idea also caused the kingship in many Celtic tribes to be passed on from the King to the son of the King's sister – at least, they argued, you would always be certain who the mother was, but not the father. It should be remembered also that King Arthur's only son was the result of a union with his stepsister. So when there was no obvious candidate for the successful King's successor, the Dark Twin himself became the Divine Substitute, and the reign could be extended a further seven years.

> The sacrifice took place in one of the Sacrificial months of the Old Religion, February, May, August or November... As he was led to his death the streets and roads were often filled with crowds, weeping, mourning, and lamenting; cloths dipped in his blood and chips of the bloodstained scaffold were carried away as sacred relics credited with healing powers. The body was dismembered and the parts distributed to different places in the country in exactly the same way as the body of the Divine King was distributed.[37]

This is all part of the pattern. A pattern which has existed for so long that it has become intrinsic to our Western inner structures in one form or another. It is a pattern which states 'that a God must die for man to live, good must deliver evil, the best of blood be shed to

---

37 Margaret Murray: *The God of the Witches*, p. 160.

redeem the worst, and the Sacrificial cycle be perpetuated to the end of time.'[38]

As was shown in the beginning of this book, the earliest pharaohs, who were manifestations of Horus in life, and Osiris in death, were thought to be ritually murdered by the Priest of Anubis at the end of an extraordinarily long period which few probably reached. No doubt this period of 28 years was the final enactment beyond which no pharaoh was allowed to rule. In the interim, he had the Apis Bull.

Osiris was the 'Bull of Amenti' (the Underworld) and, in his connection with Apis, the bull Fertility God, he became Serapis, and was intimately associated with the cycle of creation, death, and resurrection. Serapis was both a Heaven-God and God of the Underworld.

The actual bull was found in a manner reminiscent of the way the Dalai Lama is discovered: priests were appointed to search the land for a bull bearing all the necessary distinguishing marks. The bull itself was always black; there would be a triangular (or square) patch on its forehead, double hairs on its tail, and the sign of an eagle on its back, somewhere. All Egypt rejoiced when a new Apis was found. When this happened, the old bull was ritually slaughtered, its flesh eaten, and its remains mummified in the royal manner. It was finally buried with great ceremony at Saqqara, in the building known as the Serapeum.

This last was an underground structure begun in the 18th Dynasty, where the lives of the bulls were carefully recorded. In later Dynasties, the Apis bull was kept in a courtyard near the south gateway of the sanctuary of Ptah at Memphis. Here he was enthroned and honoured. His advice, presumably channelled by his priests, was eagerly sought, because he was thought to possess oracular powers. In artistic representations he was shown as a bull-headed man standing with his legs apart, wearing the Moon-disk within the crescent Moon and surmounted by two large plumes. He wore a breastplate on which were two cobras, and he carried the royal insignia of Osiris. He was Osiris incarnate – the Horned God. We know him well by now.

One of the major figures from Egyptian legends, as opposed to pure myths, was Kha'm-uast. He was the eldest son of Rameses II and high priest of Ptah in Memphis, where he was presumably the major

---

38 William Gray, *Sangreal Sacrament*. (York Beach, ME: Samuel Weiser, 1983).

channel for the Apis-spirit. This type of shamanistic role may seem inconsistent with the popular notions of Egyptian magic, but in fact it has been analysed at some length already in Billie John's brilliant exegesis of Kha'm-uast as a true Initiate.

**When I first footnoted this I made the comment 'In Preparation'. In fact her essay was expanded and became the core of our *Inner Guide to Egypt*. In some ways, the first edition of *Earth God Rising* was an act of preparation for me personally, as writing the *IGE* turned me and Billie inside out and upside down. She wrote to me in the first place because she had read my *Dancers to the Gods*, which detailed the magical work done by Christine Hartley and Kim Seymour while initiates of the Fraternity of the Inner Light in the late 1930s. Having had an inner contact with Kha'm-uast since she had been a young girl in California, it was a revelation to her that others worked with him too.**

In many ways, he was the Egyptian Merlin, a master magician of awesome powers. Had it not been for the supreme longevity of his father, he would certainly have become pharaoh – and a wondrously 'winged pharaoh' at that. As it was, apart from his role as overseer of all the religio-magical ceremonies of the Upper and Lower Kingdoms, with a status similar to that held by the Archbishop of Canterbury in England, he had the Serapeum as something akin to his own temple, where the Apis bulls and the spirit(s) behind them surrounded him daily. In death, he was actually entombed with them. Kha'm-uast, High Priest of a Horned God, was to emerge from his tomb almost three thousand years later to start teaching the art of High Magic to a whole new breed of aspirants in the 20th century. He knew how to die all right, and exactly where to die.[39]

With this reference to Archbishops, we can return with some necessity to the theme of The Divine King in England, which is the title of Margaret Murray's seminal and brilliant book. The

---

39 See Alan Richardson and Billie Walker-John: *The Inner Guide to Egypt*. Llewellyn USA

Archbishops of Canterbury, she asserted, were meant to be rather like those Dark Twins already mentioned. They were meant to hold and mediate the spiritual energies, and deal with the inner life of the nation, while at the same time they were to act, as the occasion and monarch demanded, as the Substitute.

The details of these historical relationships have been recounted extensively by Dr. Murray's admirers, so we need do no more than outline them here. It is a magical fact that if the reader really needs to learn about these Divine Kings and their Substitutes at some length, then the information itself will appear 'as if by magic' from other perfectly natural but no less surprising sources. For our present purposes, we need only say that Dr. Murray's analyses are given in convincing detail.

There was Thomas Becket, Divine Substitute for Henry II, Dunstan likewise for Edwy, Lanfranc for William the Conqueror, Anselm for Rufus, and perhaps Henry VIII's three beheaded Chancellors for him. To this, we could add Joan of Arc and Gilles de Rais, who perhaps acted in a similar capacity for the French King.

So not only Archbishops but other souls close to the King in question and probably from certain special families – 'victim' families in a sense – served in this way.

I had forgotten all this. It reads now as completely new, and also extremely seductive. Not to mention fertile. It makes my Zen garden look exactly what it is – barren. I think it was Crowley who was supposed to have exclaimed on his death-bed: *I am perplexed!* Well, on my death-bed I'd like to gasp: *I am bemused...*

I am bemused now as I get up to walk around my Zen garden widdershins, overlooking its patterns so far, trying to raise the power of my understanding. The words of an old Donovan hippy-ish song come into my head: "First there is a mountain, then there is no mountain, then there is..." As someone once said about the Wiccan movement, you start off believing everything about its 'ancient traditions', then you see them as utter rubbish, and then you realise that while they might be rubbish they still work.

Murray's thesis, to which I have given no real thought for the last two decades, suddenly appeared like an old friend whose charm I had almost forgotten. Things rise up. I can almost see the tips of the sacred oak, ash and thorn trees growing through the pebbles of my austere Zen construct; there is a shimmering in the air around it that can only come from what R.J. Stewart brilliantly termed the Primal Land. Historically the whole premise of Divine Kings and their Substitutes might well be wrong but – ye gods – it looks beautiful in there.

I suppose, rather than agonizing about whether it is a real but alternative history I should just go with the narrative flow and act 'as if', and let the sheer mythopoeic storyline stream through me again like the 'Atlantean' energies I mentioned earlier. Perhaps they are one and the same.

William G. Gray, who wrote a lot about Sacred Kings and who worked separate magic with witches such as Doreen Valiente, Pat Crowther and Robert Cochrane, never once believed in their pseudo-histories. Anyone who ever mentioned the word 'witch' or 'wicca' would have to listen to a long though brilliant lecture about how the aforementioned individuals, while being able to raise genuine power with deep insight into the otherworlds, were just misguided or downright fibbing about their provenance.

I think it took about a generation before Margaret Murray and Robert Graves' ideas really impacted upon mine, and had us all leaping deosil around the Sacred Landscapes for the Sacred Kings and their Dark Twins. Then we all began to pull back a little or in some cases reject their theses completely. And then, afresh, take the attitude that – somehow – despite the patent nonsense, it was all quite wonderful.

I do believe that tribal kings were ritually sacrificed for the reasons or impulses given. I am not sure that the system was used at the national level, but then no-one has ever disproved it. I do not believe there was any uniform, recognised Old Religion throughout Western Europe but that there were myriad tribal groups and clans for whom the idea of a Great Goddess and Horned God in differing forms was a general currency of belief.

Yes, as I said before, let us think of it all as part of the Western Mystery Tradition, into which we must find our own gnosis.

Murray cites a considerable amount of evidence for the validity of her thesis – evidence which is either derided by the orthodox historians as 'vapid balderdash,' or else unequivocally accepted by those of a more occult or unorthodox inclination. In the matter of the Sacred Kings, however, like in all occult topics, there is overwhelming evidence for those who believe but never remotely enough for those who wish to remain sceptical. Yet Dr. Murray was, I would insist, substantially correct. Her mistake – if it can be called that – was in writing purely from the point of view of the historian and anthropologist and taking no cognizance of the possibility that such patterns repeat themselves on a mythic level throughout history, without needing the back-up of covert pagan societies interweaving their rites throughout the orthodox structures of the time.

The story of Kennedy's assassination is a case in point. *The Divine King in England* perhaps fails in the author's attempt to impose her thesis beyond the Tudor dynasty, even suggesting that Oliver Cromwell, of all people, made certain agreements with the Old Religion that she felt was still ruling from behind the scenes.[40]

Still, she may have been right. She did point out, almost in passing, that certain historical personages in certain parts of Britain were more closely associated with the Divine King concepts than in others. Perhaps because the priests in those areas were more literate, and able to record it all. She referred, for example to the Os kings of Northumbria: Osbald, Osbert, Osfrith, Osred, Osric, Ostrith, Oswald, Oswin and Oswulf.

Northumbria's spiritual power was and is derived from the isle of Lindisfarne, a tiny and mystical landmass which can be reached by foot twice a day when the tide recedes. According to the magician W. E. Butler, the power-source of Britain was to be found in Glastonbury; the love-aspect of the nation's psyche was held by Iona (an island off the west coast of Scotland identified with St. Columba); and Lindisfarne was the source of the wisdom-aspect. Not everyone accepts this, but at least it provides some people with certain angles to work on. The sources of these Kings' temporal power were often divided between Bamburgh – that serpent-rock place already mentioned – or Yeavering, further inland. But they all acknowledged the peculiar sanctity of Lindisfarne.

---

40 There are people today who suggest that the mysterious death of the Duke of Kent during World War II was because he was a Divine Substitute.

*Os* is the Saxon rune ᚩ. The names of these Northumbrian kings were thus to be regarded as titles: Osbald – Bold God; Osbert – Bright God; Oswulf – Divine Wolf, and so on. Os was thus a reference to the God, as far as they were concerned, a specific identification with Odin – he of the one eye and the Wild Hunt, who found his wisdom in the tree Yggdrasil whose branches conceal four harts. They held Odin within their names in the same way that pharaohs took on the syllables of Osiris. In this last factor we find a sonic coincidence that fits our scheme perfectly.

But these were obscure figures, admittedly little kings from a small realm. To get onto more national levels, and those with international and eternal relevance, we have to look at some of the larger figures in history.

What must be realized first is that in medieval times Britain was a multi-ethnic society, much as America is today. At varying times, the inhabitants comprised Angles, Saxons, Jutes, and the Brythonic and Goidelic Celts, who were to sort themselves out as the Scottish, Irish, Welsh, and Cornish peoples – all with their own variants of Celtic tongues. These were interlaced with people of Roman origin who were likely to have come from any part of the vast Roman Empire and who regarded themselves as the true aristocrats regardless of what hard times they may have fallen on after the legions left. Then there were regular and substantial influxes of refugees, traders, travellers from Brittany, Normandy, the Holy Land, and, generally speaking, all points east of Dover and south of the Isle of Wight and north of Lindisfarne.

The very name England was said to derive from the god Ing, who has been equated with the fertility God, Freyr. His twin sister and sometimes consort, Freya, or Frigga, is often depicted riding on a broomstick, or a cat.[41]

The English became a homogeneous people only slowly, and only after the momentous Battle of Hastings in 1066. After this Norman Conquest, it was never invaded again until World War II when something like a million G.I.s came to delight our womenfolk with their bubblegum, bucks and – as many satisfied females were happy to imply – their apparently insatiable sexual appetites. The Battle of Hastings put the lid on a melting-pot, just as Ankh-f-n-Khonsu once

---

41 It is from this goddess that we get the sexual term 'frig'.

put the seal upon an Aeon. Hastings was the enactment between nations of the kind that should really have only occurred between the Twins.

When one man tries to sustain his power and dynasty at an unnaturally high and unyielding peak, and when he creates laws, armies and societies which all have the perpetuation of this power as their sole aim, then war is the inevitable result. War is a perversion of the Horned God's rule, even if it is sometimes necessary and tinged with the justice of Maat. War spills the blood of the common man upon the ground to ensure the continuation of the King and the King's seed, and the King's status. But the Divine King spills his own blood upon the ground for the furtherance of his people and their seed – and, in the purely agricultural sense, of their seeds.

Hastings was a conflict that was never inevitable, or even necessary, but it imposed grave changes upon the world. It was a conflict that was, perhaps, not so much about land and wealth and lust – although all of these played prominent parts – but about a religion that was quite new, and another that was indeed very old. Therein lay the real battles.

Americans take heed. One way or another it will happen there too, although on inner rather than outer levels.

**I have no idea what I was talking about with that last sentence. Sorry.**

**However I recall, years ago, someone advancing the argument that if the Normans and their Rome-ish attitudes toward women had not triumphed in 1066, then women in England would have had full equality by about the 13th Century. Also, on that note, one of my other selves, Ywi, has often burbled acidly that if 'Saint' Wilfrid had not triumphed at the Synod of Whitby and thus brought the Northumbrian church into the mainstream of Roman culture, then we might have seen women priests and women bishops of the Celtic Christians secure in their tenures by the 8th Century. And I think it was the deliciously provocative writer Ralph Ellis who raged that if the Early Church had not destroyed all the libraries of the known world then we might have had space flight centuries ago, instead of being plunged into the woman-hating Dark Ages.**

Edward the Confessor is a good enough figure to start with: lean and lugubrious, tart, and often melancholy, with enough culture, elegance, sanctity and religion to make everyone suspect that he was not the paragon of Anglo-Saxon manhood. In no way did he fulfil any of the criteria for being the Horned God's representative on Earth – for, despite his marriage, he was a complete failure between the sheets. The marriage was almost certainly a chaste one, and toward the end of his life he spoke of his young wife in such glowing terms that none of his contemporaries could doubt that he had never touched her.

The cult of the Sacred King had probably ceased in England by this time. He was never 'sacred' in the Pagan sense of the term. It may have ceased a generation before him, even, by the time of King Cnut, known more popularly as Canute.

This was the king who was supposed to have tried to command the waves as an act of madness. But the truth of it was that Cnut (a very decent king) was actually trying to show his courtiers that he was not divine, but a mere mortal, and that the tide would wet his feet like those of any man. The first schoolboy version shows Cnut as an idiot; the second adult revision portrays Cnut's people as idiots. Perhaps he was just trying to show that no matter what they had been used to with previous kings, and no matter what they expected, he, Cnut, a Danish King ruling England, was not a God. Not for him were the sacrificial death or the apparently cruel gods of the Old Religion.

That is one possibility. Details are so scarce that, by use of those magical words 'perhaps,' 'possibly,' 'may have been' and 'it may well be,' we can turn it into what we want.

But there was no mistaking Edward's vision on his deathbed, which was recorded carefully by his attendants. They did this partly because he had a reputation for visions and minor miracles, but also because they were desperate for some sort of clue as to who his successor should be. As he slipped in and out of his delirium during January of 1065, he had one dream/vision which had enough impact to rouse him into a few final moments of lucidity.

In this, he saw two long-dead monks he had known years before in Normandy. They were warning him that, because of the wickedness of the earls and churchmen of England, the country was about to be cursed: Devils would ride through the land with fire and sword and war. God would only cease to punish England when a green tree,

## ... and the places of sacrifice ...

felled halfway up its trunk and the top part taken three furlongs away, would join itself together again by its own efforts, without the aid of man, and break into leaf and fruit again.

His attendants looked hard at each other and had much discussion later. Yet surely it was not entirely symbolic. Edward had spent many of his younger years in Normandy, and he had said just enough to his hosts to suggest that the throne might, just might, go to the Duke of Normandy. His final words of warning, I would suggest, had less to do with clairvoyance than with a clear knowledge of the sort of man the Duke of Normandy was, and of the sort of God – or in his eyes, Devil – that the man and all his forebears followed.

William the Bastard was the son of Robert the Devil – nicknames which did not offend the bearers in the slightest. It was recorded that, at the end of the 10$^{th}$ century or at the beginning of the 11th, the Devil, in the likeness of the Duke of Normandy, came to the Duke's wife in a wood, and as a result of this union, she bore a son who was known as Robert the Devil.

We have a sense of *déjà vu* here. Surely this is another aspect of that semi-divine shape-changing which results in someone rather special. Uther did this with Ygraine; Nephthys did this with Osiris. The Duke's wife, we might imagine, was in the wood in the first place to do more than gather berries. She was there for the sacred mating, the *hieros gamos*. It was the Horned God's representative upon earth with whom she mated.

Robert the Devil in turn married a woman known as Herleve, or Arlette, the daughter of a tanner in the town of Falaise, but by the time of the ceremony they had already had a son, William the Bastard, a name which he bore as a simple description of his status.

William the Bastard himself was to marry a woman named Matilda. All her other qualities apart, Matilda is worth mentioning here if only because of her size. When her tomb was opened in 1967 she was found to be just over four feet tall. Was she one of the fays?

The Normans as a people were, like the English, partly of Viking stock, although England had been invaded mainly by Danish Vikings, while Normandy received the brunt of Viking invasions from Norway. The differences between the two nations were marked: England was as settled and stable a country as any in Europe could be, whereas the Normans at that time were swept up by the primitive cults of horsemanship and war which would, in the following century, take shape as that international brotherhood known as Chivalry, under which the great romances were about to be created.

It is said, with some degree of truth, that every nation gets the sort of leader it deserves. England had The Confessor to act as an incarnation of its spirit. The Normans had The Bastard. Born in the year 1027 or 1028, William was a man who was rigid, cruel and powerful, and who cared nothing about what people thought. Probably illiterate, he had all the diplomatic niceties and the political refinements of Attila the Hun. Even if he did, on occasion, resort to Christian law to gain support for his schemes, he was in no sense of the word a Christian.

When Edward the Confessor died, William was actually staggered to hear that, far from the English proclaiming him as the new king and eagerly lining the shores awaiting his triumphant arrival, they had actually crowned someone else in his place! He did the only thing he understood well: he gathered his army and prepared for war …

The crown of England had actually been claimed by Harold Godwinson, who was everyone's favourite, the complete opposite of The Bastard. Harold was patient, kind, charismatic, learned – and as hard a fighting man as could be found anywhere in the world. He was the leader of the house-carls, a small and professional army of men who were so tough that even a saga from Norway, homeland of the Vikings, told how one English house-carl was worth two soldiers from anywhere else in the world. They fought on foot, with swords and two-handed axes. And, with their backing, Harold prepared for the invasion he knew would surely come – not just from William in the south but from Tostig in the north, who was Harold's half-brother and yet another rival to the throne.

The rest of the story is clear enough. Harold, waiting for the Norman fleet along the length of the southern English coastline, received news that Tostig and a massive Viking army had landed in the northeast. After a heroic march, his tired and outnumbered army nevertheless massacred the enemy, devastating them so completely that centuries of Viking raiding ended at that moment, on the bloody fields at Stamford Bridge.

Harold and his army had no sooner sat down to lick their wounds than they heard the bad tidings which proclaimed that The Bastard's army had landed on the beaches near Hastings, some 300 miles to the south. Already exhausted, they made that journey, on foot, within five days.

The Bastard won, of course. The world knows that now. But only just, barely, and only because the English had little strength left after Stamford Bridge, let alone the long marches before and after, and because the Normans had luck. They had also re-discovered the stirrup, which enabled them to fight from horseback in a way that the house-carls could not match.

And then, Sacred King claiming his rightful crown or not, The Bastard and his armies proceeded to loot, burn, and murder with an intensity that no-one, least of all the existing worshippers of the Old Gods, could have believed possible. That part of him, we might believe, was never a true expression of the Horned God.

As for Harold Godwinson, how should we regard him? Elected King? A true Christian King? Or someone just quick to seize a chance? Whichever, there are mysteries about him and his origins which are not easily resolved, given the scanty documentation. But what is certain is that, with this terrible battle, this spilling of Norman blood upon English soil for the purpose of a holy war, a link was created between the egregores of the two nations – still today, natural enemies. This link has joined them in a manner akin to the way the Bright and Dark Twins of yore were connected.

**In primordial times there was no sea between Britain and France and they shared, of course, the same rock strata. If we could, in some sense, reach that bedrock under the sea of our national consciousness, then we would reach a common level in which things Gallic would seep into our visions and dreams. I adore France and get completely exasperated by that nation. I make regular attempts to learn the language but never get much further than Restaurant French.**

We can attribute two nice touches to William, however, before we move on to study his son as an unquestionable example of a Divine

King. When he first set foot on the English beach, he sprawled his length before his omen-conscious and aghast followers. Undaunted, he rose and cried, 'By God's splendour, I have seized the soil of England in both my hands!' In fact, he did this deliberately, echoing Julius Caesar who had said the same when landing in Africa. Three hundred years after William, King Edward was to echo both of them when he landed in Normandy on his way to slaughter the French at Crécy. While in 1944, on the Normandy beachheads – the choice of which had at least been partly suggested to the Allied commanders by Winston Churchill, who thought it historically apt – the same deliberate sprawl and same words were to be exclaimed by General George Patton, who was a man wracked by more than a few mystical notions himself.

William knew that he was the focus of destiny at that moment, on the beach near Hastings where Aleister Crowley would one day go to die. He knew that he could make his omens. Some people have the knack of being able to see the future in the short term; others have the ability to shape it.

The second touch was that William had the pieces of Harold's body (had it been ritually dismembered?) wrapped in a purple cloth and buried under a heap of stones on a cliff-top overlooking the Channel. A stone was put on this simple grave bearing the following epitaph:

> By command of the Duke, you rest here a King, O Harold
> That you may be guardian still of the shore and sea.

That, as one commentator rather snootily put it, was certainly not a Christian act. 'One is left to guess that bond the burial signified between William and his nation, what old, pre-Christian magic he felt he had to propitiate.'[42]

It was the gods of the nation the new king had to deal with first: the people, he would attend to later. Pagan or not, he was a terrible, terrible man.

The true symbols of the Divine King are all to be found more clearly in William Rufus, and less speculation is needed in his case because the documentation has survived in enough detail to support the thesis. But one final thing that must be considered about that

---

42 David Haworth, *1066: The Year of the Conquest.*

period of time of William the Conqueror is his creation of what became known as the New Forest, at the end of the 11$^{th}$ Century.

The forest itself, with all its scattered villages and isolated dwellings, already existed, of course. William's 'new' forest involved not so much the planting of trees as the complete and savage extermination of the existing inhabitants and the implementation of unbelievably harsh laws against trespassers. This was all so that the New Forest could become an exclusively royal hunting ground – the chief prey being the stag. Stags have always, in Europe at least, been royal animals. The people could certainly see within the behaviour of stags a fine model of human kingship, in which the dominant stag is challenged yearly for the leadership of the herd in combats which were more ceremonial than actual. They roamed free within the New Forest, and they were hunted by the King.

The Egyptians, who lived in a narrow land with strict limits to its fertile boundaries, had the Serapeum as the home of their Sacred Bull, which was a living representative of the pharaoh and thus their God. Moved by the same impulse, though in very different forms, the New Forest was a vast and natural version of the Serapeum where the royal deer – never creatures for captivity – could run free and yet be available for the sacred rites of the King.

Even today, the New Forest, crisscrossed as it inevitably is by roads and heavy traffic, still retains its 'witchy' reputation. Indeed, its influence upon the West has not really been considered fully. Samuel Liddell Mathers, the genius behind the Hermetic Order of the Golden Dawn, was born and brought up in what were then small towns on the edge of the New Forest. A generation after him came Gerald Brousseau Gardner, whom many regard as being the major influence in bringing Witchcraft back into the world again, and who received his initiation into the Craft in the Mill House near Highcliffe, at the hands of Dorothy Clutterbuck.[43]

These two men, 'coming to magic' on the edge of the New Forest, generated two streams of light that have illuminated us all. Any modern magician who has ever studied the Qabalah, or 'risen on the planes,' or made the Enochian Calls, or used the banishing ritual of the pentagram; any witch who has ever adored the Book of Shadows,

---

[43] For the full and true story read Professor Ronald Hutton's superbly incisive but continually sympathetic *The Triumph of the Moon*.

called down the Moon, or drawn circles with the athame, owes a debt of some sort and at some level to these two men. There was Mathers, in whose Order the supreme ritual involved him assuming the God-form of Osiris and rising from the coffin to awaken the inner mind of the candidate for initiation. And there was Gardner, amazed to find that those rites of the Horned God, assumed forgotten for centuries, were in fact being practiced within some English glades. Beyond them, and binding them, were the vibrant forces of the New Forest, which covers an area considerably less than that of any moderately sized American city. Beyond that is the image of the appalling man who made it.

One day America will have its own Mathers, its own Crowley, its own Gardner and Dion Fortune. It will have its own Bastard too, and medieval patterns will work themselves out from the hearts of its own countryside, and worlds and futures will be formed because of this.

**I shudder at how patronising that sounds. As soon as I have finished this I intend to ritually scourge myself using a pink feather (consecrated of course!) as Gardner loved to do. A deep apology to all American readers. We have nothing to teach you.**

It was also in the New Forest that William Rufus, known as William the Red to those less scholarly, met his clearly sacrificial death as an Incarnate God of the Old Religion. If his father had made many enemies among the people by his method of re-imposing the Old Ways with a sword, then the wounds had been healed by the time Rufus arranged to die on their behalf while hunting a stag.

They came to his funeral in their masses. The common folk adored him ...

William Rufus was born in 1056 and crowned King of England in 1087. He was an open mocker of Christian shrines and made a hobby of destroying their churches. He was a King who dealt with law-breakers and villains of any sort with the kind of ferocity that would have made

••• and the places of sacrifice •••

Edward the Confessor faint. But he was one who at least, as the old dream goes, made the country safe for women to walk out alone at night. That was some King. He was the sort of King who exemplified the notion that 'severity, consistently applied, breeds less discontent in the kingdom than mercy randomly administered.' Never one to forget a good deed done to him or able to forgive a wrong one, he knew that he was able to justify all things in the eyes of his people by the fact that he was going to die the Old Way – a death which he finally approached with all the courage of a samurai.

On the eve of Lammas, which today is August 1st, sacred to the Bright God of Summer, William stayed awake all night chatting to his chamberlains. On the fateful morning, he dressed carefully and spent the early hours arranging his affairs, eating and drinking well and heartily. As he was being dressed for the hunt, a smith brought him six new quarrels – the short and stubby arrows used in the crossbow. Smiling, he handed two of them to Sir Walter Tyrrel, saying: 'It is right that the sharpest arrows be given to him who knows how to deal deadly strokes with them.' And then later, to the same man, he said with real gravity of manner: 'Walter, do thou justice according to those things that thou hast heard!' To which Tyrrel nodded and replied: 'So I shall, my lord.'

In the forest – that New Forest which had been all but cleared of any unnecessary inhabitants – the King became a leader of the hunt indeed: the Wild Hunt which sought himself and no other. It was not until the sun was setting that a suitable stag was seen, and William's bowstring broke. He then cried to Tyrrel: 'Draw, draw your bow for the Devil's sake and let fly your arrow, or it will be the worse for you.' Tyrrel did, and the arrow pierced the King. On being hit, the King uttered not a word but broke off the shaft where it projected on his body and fell upon the wound, which hastened his death.

According to one account, the body was found by a charcoal burner, placed in a rough cart, covered with a poor, ragged cloak and taken to Winchester, which was then one of the sacred cities of England, and probably had a population in the low thousands at most. In this account, great emphasis was placed upon the image of the King's blood dripping onto the ground during the whole journey – and although this is not possible it emphasizes the belief that the blood of the Divine King must fall upon the ground to fertilize it.

Rufus was not mourned by the nobles or ecclesiastics of that church he had so mocked in his lifetime, but by the common people. The poor, the widows and the beggars came out in great numbers to meet the funeral procession and follow the King to his grave. It was their dead King, who had been the incarnation of their God, and the true regent of the common man.

His death was known in Europe within hours. No-one is sure how this happened, although a Roman Legion-type signalling system has been suggested. Perhaps it was because they all knew he had to die at the appointed hour. Perhaps, with the elements of shamanism certainly active at that time, other communities simply knew, just as Aboriginal tribespeople even today can know that one of their members has had an accident, even hundreds of miles away. I knew when my mother died, on the other side of the country – a common enough experience.[44] As an Englishman, I would expect to know about the death of my King.[45] Certainly there is the tale – a hint to the common folk and fays – that the Earl of Cornwall, while walking in the New Forest, met a large hairy goat carrying the body of the dead King on its back. When questioned, the goat replied that it was carrying the corpse to the Devil for judgment. Here, surely, we can see a distorted version of the Horned God's priest in his ritual robes carrying the corpse away for the ritual dismemberment and/or feast.

We have to remember, too, that most of these were written down by clerics who would naturally interpret pagan rites in their own terms. When William cried: 'Draw your bow for the Devil's sake!' We may be sure he was using the name of his own God, who Dr. Murray thinks may well have been Loki. Now Loki was once one of the supreme Gods of the Norsemen, but came to share that fate common to all Gods of his sparkling but darkling nature when he was later seen as a creature of pure evil.

There was pagan blood in Rufus, all right. Whatever crimes had been committed in England by his forebears were expiated by his sacrificial act. As we are learning, the old saying 'blood will out' has significance in more ways than we could have imagined before. We can leave the sacrificial genealogies of England to other writers

---

44 That is completely untrue.
45 That is complete bollocks.

••• and the places of sacrifice •••

who have already gone over this ground in exhaustive detail. In the magical way of things, those readers who actually need such detail will find the books in question.

The whole concept of the Sacred Kingship based upon carefully preserved bloodlines has been given a notable boost recently by *Holy Blood, Holy Grail*, a best-selling and highly controversial book which has, in fact, done no more than state publicly what many occultists had been saying for most of their lives: that Jesus did not die upon the cross, that he married Mary Magdalen, that they had children. According to the authors Baigent, Green and Leigh, this secret dynasty was protected and nurtured by the mysterious Prieuré de Sion, an organization with (we are led to believe) enormous influence in the highest places, and a talent down through the ages for manipulating history.

We need not look with too much awe upon the Prieuré. Really, when we study the dark and furious history of Europe we can only conclude that the history-manipulators of the Prieuré were largely inept. Whatever glamour it might seem to possess can be banished at once with three simple words: Belsen, Dachau, Auschwitz.

**As Lynn Picknett and Clive Prince (not to mention dozens of others) have shown,[46] the whole notion of the Priory of Sion was always largely fanciful, even if there are still many intriguing mysteries connected with Rennes le Château. I'm glad I never got sucked too far into that one. I think this is a case of researchers digging down into those strata which unite Britain and France and finding all sorts of weird things glowing toward them.**

**Even as I write this I see news bursting about a fragment of (apparently) provenly ancient manuscript called *The Gospel of Jesus's Wife* which is upsetting the Catholic Church just a little because it states boldly that he was married, and that his wife would become a priest. While this synchronicity is pleasing, I have found after thousands of such happenings in my everyday life, synchronicities often don't mean a damned thing. After years of regarding them as Signs, and following the (usually fruitless) leads they seemed to provide, the best I can look at them now is as 'meaninglessly meaningful' or 'meaningfully**

---

46 *The Sion Revelation*

meaningless'. Like small static electrical shocks you can get if you walk on the wrong type of carpet with the wrong type of shoes.

It is a question, also, of whether we accept Jesus as the Son of God, or a Son of Light. This in itself points out a peculiar advantage enjoyed by Pagans that not many of them realize: By regarding Jesus as *a* Son of Light – one of many – they can actually work with and appreciate much of the Christian Mystery Tradition while at the same time they never need to surrender their own pantheons. Christians, on the other hand, must necessarily accept the exclusivity of their God, and are forever denied the use of Pagan altars.

It was because the followers of the Old Religion saw in the image of Jesus another example of a Divine King and Sacrificed God that they were quite happy let the new religion put down roots. To polytheists, or pantheists, one more Son of Light would not make much difference to their world. And Jesus, as a Thorned God, was just one more in a long line of such beings, even if he did ascend via his Father in Heaven rather than descend to the Underworld/Otherworld/Place of Ancestors as true Horned Gods invariably had to do. If the actual sacrifice, entailing the spilling of blood on the ground, was crucial to the mystery, it was equally supported by the necessity of the 'divine dismemberment' which followed.

Just as Osiris' body was cut into fourteen pieces, and each piece buried in a different part of his kingdom, so can we find a very similar process at work in England – particularly as regards the head, which was regarded as the most sacred thing of all. When King Oswald of Northumbria was defeated in battle, his head was removed and placed first in the churchyard at Lindisfarne, and later removed to Durham. His body meanwhile was taken to Bordeaux in France, and then later back home to Gloucester. Somehow one of his arms found its way to Peterborough – that town where the first recorded sighting of the Wild Hunt was made – and it was described as being 'whole of flesh.' This is a common theme for all dead and mystical heroes – their bodies do not decay. Like Egyptian mummies, they remain whole and uncorrupted.

## ... and the places of sacrifice ...

In fact, some of the kings were actually embalmed, although the process was by no means as sophisticated as that practiced in Egypt. When Henry I died, all his internal organs were removed, the head was removed to extract the brain (the Egyptians did so via the nasal passages, using drills and hooks), and the eyes were also taken out. The head was then sewn on the neck, the corpse wrapped in ox-hides and taken to Caen, and from there back to England to be buried at Reading.

A similar fate was recorded for Richard I, King John, Henry V and probably many others, including Catherine of Aragon, who, Margaret Murray speculates, was one of the women who refused to become a Substitute for the King. (It was left to Ann Boleyn to do this, a firm product of the Old Religion, who willingly redeemed Catherine's lack of faith.)

The parallels between the English and Egyptian systems are not exact, however, and admittedly these may be circumstantial anyway. For one thing, England was never as united as the Old Land. In an ideal realm, in Avalon, the body of the King would be broken into 13 pieces (in Egypt, 14) and scattered throughout the 13 parts of the kingdom. Yet we can contrive to see a possibility of this pattern in the 13 monastic cathedrals served by regular clergy or monks. These are:

| | |
|---|---|
| Bristol | Norwich |
| Carlisle | Oxford |
| Chester | Peterborough |
| Durham | Rochester |
| Ely | Winchester |
| Gloucester | Worcester |
| Canterbury | |

We could gloss over this but for the fact that Peterborough is again so prominent. This is the place where the dismembered parts of Kings and their notional Substitutes are to be found, and where the Wild Hunt was seen. At the time of writing this, in a purely synchronistic, or 'magical' coincidence, news has appeared that archaeologists working at an industrial estate at Peterborough have unearthed weapons, jewellery and skeletons almost 3000 years old, which show the site to have one of the largest sacrificial centres in prehistoric Europe.

Were all of those other cathedrals located at places which had major magical significance in an era long before the Christians came? Doubtless this was so. That was the Christian way.

The process of dismemberment, and the distribution of the parts to areas or individuals as a means of bringing luck and fertility, is not so far removed from the modern soul. There is a woman in a nearby town who has, she insists, one of Elvis Presley's toe-nails, found on a visit to Graceland. She now preserves it like it was the Holy Grail itself. People today seek autographs and other mementos with the same intensity that their forebears sought locks of hair, or limbs, and for the same reason: as a means of relating to something special, something or someone greater than themselves. In so doing they manage to feel they too have become elevated toward the 'stars.'

All of this may seem far removed from the daily concerns of today, but, as C. G. Jung said: 'Everything old is a sign of something coming.' We must look beyond the mere events to find the universal patterns within them, and thus touch those royal and divine aspects within ourselves.

There is nothing intrinsically sacred about the Englishness of the historical events just described, for the patterns occur among all peoples in all lands. But they were at least put down on paper and recorded. This enables us to roll the details into crystal spheres for our own convenience and thus use the essence of history as a vehicle for prophecy. It is not infallible (prophecy never is) and is often relevant to no one beyond the individual, but it is a means of unlocking energies that will ultimately go beyond the individual and across the years.

Even the details of divine dismemberment and the places of storage can provide us with magic, for we can all try to link our associate parts with portions of the landscape. We can do this at a local level, such as apparently happened in the ancient Goddess-centre of Avebury in Wiltshire, whereby the streams, valleys, hills and numberless megalithic remains were all expressions of the Goddess in her cycles from Maiden, Mother to Crone. Or we can play our game again, trying to do this at a national level by identifying where a country's brain centre is, or heart-centre, and so on.

We already do this unconsciously when we describe a particular place as being the 'arm-pit' of the state, or even the arsehole of an area. A crude game, perhaps, but one which can yield surprising results. We can also – and should also – do this within our lives: 'My heart is in [N] because I grew up there; my head is in [N] because that was where I learned most; my strength is in [N] because I learned toughness there; and so on. In this sense, we have to think in terms of qualities rather than physical bits and pieces: compassion is your left arm, discipline your right; career is your torso; and so forth.

There can be no hard and fast rules to this, for you have to become your own Wild Hunt, chase yourself, and pull yourself apart. Some people, already torn asunder by life, have to become their own Isis in search of their own parts and learn to pull themselves together again.

This is the real magic, the true sorcery. We are all daily practitioners of the Old Religion if we could only see it. The spirit of Divine Kings is within us all.

---

**Now, a generation after writing all this, the quantum-history of Divine and Sacred Kings won't quite die. I use that term because if everything that can happen does happen, then there are ways and realms in which Margaret Murray's and Robert Graves' notions were/are exquisitely true.**

**If my generation leapt upon a spiritual bandwagon, there seems to be a new generation today (2017) which talks about Prince Charles, with all his long-held eco-warrior, conservationist, global warming fears and passion for the land, being somehow 'Special', a true manifestation of Arthur (which is one of his middle names). Diana, they insist, was chosen to mate with him because of her much older Spencer blood-line, which carries within her DNA all sorts of ancient and potent possibilities for her children, and that her first child William is the Once and Future King.**

**I make no judgement on this.**

# THE TIME OF THE WAKENING

The Old Religion never really died, as so many thought. Christianity never really triumphed in any absolute sense. What happened was that the Horned Gods and Goddesses of each region 'passed on' in the truly magical, rather than the purely euphemistic, sense. In mythological terms, they disappeared into the hills, just as the fays went into their mounds, and just as humanity today (if the worst thing happens) will take to the nuclear bunkers. Like Osiris, the Horned God took up his place within the Underworld. There he waits for the True Son to claim his helm and perform a sort of 'Ritual of the Opening of the Mouth', whereby the ancient energies would spring forth again from the Otherworlds.

The Horned God and his rites and representatives withdrew by necessity. Conditions on the land were changing rapidly. This perhaps was coupled with the increasing development of that left-brain consciousness unable to perceive the natural forces and the ancestors as having direct and living impact upon the individual. Christianity, acting as something of the Dark Twin, did no more than rip out the heart of an already dying sacrifice.

We could blame the introduction of the heavy ploughs, which could accomplish in one day what it would normally take many men a whole week to achieve. We could blame Pietro de Crescenzi for his *Opus ruralium commodorum* (1304), which showed man how to control the land by means other than magical propitiation, and at the same time we could direct some animosity toward John Fitzherbert for developing these ideas in his book, *Husbandry*. Later still, we could rail against the likes of Messrs. Tull and Meikle, whose seed-planting machines and threshing machines completely revolutionised the harvest. Or we could blame the plagues which devastated perhaps as much as half the population of England alone, and altered the fabric of society forever. Or else we might cast a cold eye on those agricultural developments that took the small plots of land away from the subsistence farmers and concentrated them in the hands of a few powerful land-owning individuals who left the rest to machines.

But most of all, in England at least, we can blame the sheep. The demand for English wool was so great, and so much money was to be made from it, that vast areas of hitherto inhabited and cultivated land were turned over to the grazing of sheep. This meant that the bulk of the population was driven off the land and into the cities, causing Thomas More to exclaim that: 'The sheep have eaten up the men!'[47] Natural cycles were forgotten; communities that had once achieved a precious (and often precarious) self-sufficiency through a kind of symbiosis with the land and its seasons were destroyed. Forests were levelled to make yet more land for grazing. In time, the international demand for wool was to have as much impact upon once-Merrie England as the discovery of oil was to have upon the Arab nations.

The Christians, who used the Lamb as their totem animal, and who now saw the Old Religion retreating everywhere, must have been well pleased. They did their very best with the noose and the burning faggots to help the process along.

It is at this period that we can catch glimpses of the Horned God and his Goddess in full flight. Herne/Gwyn, call him what you will, was reviled as the Foul Fiend, the Enemy of Salvation and a true Lord of Darkness. His influence was seen as malignant and deadly; corruption and putrefaction were thought to mark his every step. And no one could see that this was a symptom of the ways in which Man's relationship with Nature had become corrupted – it was in this relationship that the real putrefaction laid. A few places still did persevere with the old worship. The clerical authorities made clear these were orgiastic ceremonies in which the Devil and his Whore were adored, and at which unspeakable sacrifices were made.

Three processes were at work here:

First is that attitude already mentioned in which a society and its priests had lost touch with the sensuous yet innocent and joyous

---

[47] Saint Thomas More was the scourge of heretics. What was their heresy? They translated the Bible into English.

aspects of the old Fertility Cult, so that the image of a free and running stag, for example, became corrupted into the static and all-consuming goat which best exemplified the Christian interpretation.

Second, we can see the ultimate development of that technique of religious conversion whereby which the gods of the former religion become the devils of the new.

Third, it is true to say that some of the covens were actually involved in calling on forces of real darkness. Divorced from the old cycles of Nature, living in a distraught world where the tribes and (later) agricultural communities no longer existed, they sought wealth and power, pleasure through whatever magical means beckoned them, using whatever techniques were deemed most potent.

This 'corruption of images' can be seen in different ways. If the Royal Family of medieval England was no longer seen as Divine, and no longer acted out the great rituals, then members of the lesser nobility often took a Witch King mantle upon themselves. Presumably this was done through a kind of despairing Apostolic Succession down through the ranks. Thus Francis Stewart, Fifth Earl of Bothwell, the nephew of Mary Queen of Scots, was rumoured to have been the very incarnation of the witches' Dark Lord. Bothwell was indeed a very dark man; if he was a true King of the Witches, it was a mantle he did not deserve.

The idea of living sacrifices offered to the Horned God is also a corruption of a far older and purer truth linked with that deity. This is not at all to be confused with the notion of Willing Sacrifice described in the previous chapter. The truth is simply that the Horned God will give things, but he will also take something away. This is the cosmic Law of Exchange, which says, in simple terms: If you want something, you have to pay for it somehow. Matter can neither be created nor destroyed – it can only be swapped around a bit. Not only had humanity lost the living essence of their oldest God in the later centuries, it lost this knowledge concerning the exchange of spiritual energies. If we want things from the Horned God – knowledge, love, power – then we must be careful to consider what we might offer him from within ourselves in return. It is the subtlety of this exchange that holds many of the secrets of his awakening today.

It was Bobbie Gray who told me that. When I remember her she is always in mannish clothes, standing in the doorway leading into Bill's little study, like a chain-smoking gate-keeper into the Mysteries. All she actually said was: "The Horned God will give, but he will also take away." That single sentence had an enormous impact on me and played no small part in bringing through this book as a whole.

It leads onto the Horus/Set synergy: your invocations might suffuse you with Light, but as long as you are in the material world then Shadow will also be created. However, inverting this, whenever you find yourself drenched in darkness you must use it to find the light behind the obstacles causing it.

Look at all the personal and historical examples when attempts to do something wholly positive have brought unintended or unforeseen consequences. And vice versa.

This intuitive knowledge had all but disappeared by the time of the 18th and 19th centuries, although a few individuals in remote parts of the countryside still possessed the sort of natural magical powers which singled them out as witches. In visual terms, the only hints in the world that there had ever been anything other than a Thorned God were to be found in the 'foliate heads.'

These are church-carvings in which a human face is seen peeping through foliage, or a face actually formed from foliage, or one with foliage sprouting from the mouth in a wonderfully Osirian manner. They could be found carved on roof bosses, corbels, capitals, fonts, tympana, tombs, and on wooden screens, bench-ends, and misericords, and so on. All are likely to be seen in any church with pre-1500 features. It is as though the stone-carvers were determined to remember this figure from the Old Worship even if no one else was.[48]

These faces were all that remained, at least in England, of that divine figure who had once brought fertility to the land.

---

[48] Janet and Colin Bord, *Earth-rites: Fertility practices in pre-industrial Britain*. (London: Collins, 1983).

Why did I not mention the Sheila-na-Gigs? These were carvings of naked women, squatting with legs apart, triumphantly exposing their own vulva. They were often placed discreetly above doors or windows in churches, presumably to protect these openings.

Modern scholars differ in their interpretations. Anne Ross and Maureen Concannon were certain that these carvings depicted the war-goddess or the mother goddess respectively, while to Mircea Eliade the figures represented the goddess who granted kingship. Perhaps, as with the foliate heads, it was a means of hinting to the common folk sitting in the pews, taking part in rituals that used a Latin tongue they could not understand, that there was always Another Way.

And – who knows? – maybe there really was a secretive Old Religion after all.

These, and all those folk-customs which even the English themselves thought quaint, were like the last reverberations of a once-powerful cry – the cry of the rutting stag which goes *Her-Her-Hernaa, Hernaaa...*[49]

There was Morris Dancing and maypole dancing, ceremonies which involved circling churches or tapping on trees to awaken them, little springtime rites (often now with the full blessing of a secure and ignorant Church). Many of these customs related to springs and wells and orchards, and the frequent appearance of some local who was called 'Jack in the Green' or the 'Green Man,' and who appeared in a variety of strangely Osirian forms; for example, in a wicker pyramid, or all covered in vegetation, or smeared in black as Osiris was black when he was found in the silt of the Nile. All these things were like those memories which stick maddeningly on the tip of the tongue, impossible to place, but with intense and evocative flavours nevertheless.

It is with the title 'Green Man' that we find ourselves most surely full circle, back to those impossibly distant days in the First Time, as they called it, when Osiris was the Green Man who taught his people how to raise crops, cultivate vines, and make peace – that best of all.

---

49 Observed by Doreen Valiente.

### ••• the time of the wakening •••

Here was the true son of the Earth God who contained within himself the patterns of birth, growth, death, and renewal on all levels, and in all ways. Here was the figure that held the secret and source of fertility, both within the land and within the people who worked that land. Sometimes, in small villages along the Nile, they would honour him by fastening heads on poles – heads made from corn and adorned with hair, feathers, and horns – in a reverential act that was no different from the folk-customs involving corn-dollies in old England, several thousand years later.

Whether we focus upon Herne or upon Osiris, in both cases their relationships are concerned with involving humanity in a direct and living relationship with the Earth, in particular with the specific geographies in which individuals conduct their lives, whether these are in the depths of the city or the heart of the forest.

*An Osiris bed found in Tutankhamun's tomb*

They can both teach us about the 'spirit of place,' and show us how we can learn from this to find the 'place of spirit,' and so take our positions in the dance of nature from which we have become sadly separated. They teach us the spiritual law: as without, so within – there is no difference.

The fate of the earth itself hangs on how we learn to deal with the energies they focus. We are at that moment in time when Horus is visiting the inert and listless figure of his father who is lost within the Underworld and guarded (and also constrained) by monstrous serpents. His father, remember, has that 'wound in the thigh' which has somehow been responsible for the wasteland in which he now lives. Horus is there to claim his crown as the Earth-God's true heir, but first he must perform that crucial ceremony known as 'The Opening of the Mouth,' using a small adze to help him. Once the mouth is opened, the life of the world will spring forth, as with the foliate heads, and a new cycle will begin. Osiris transcends his helplessness – he lives, and the Earth lives with him.

As above, so below – Horus and Osiris in balance.

Part of the ceremony involves Horus telling Osiris exactly what ails him. Osiris cannot be cured until that is done. It presupposes that the son is mature enough, and knowledgeable enough, to be able to speak with certainty about the world's ills.

Today, as we look upon our polluted oceans, breathe our polluted atmosphere and watch the destruction of those natural resources vital to the ecosystem, we find the Horus-hawk alive within us, and horrified.

It is a start. It is *the* start.

But a cure for this land of waste and pollution cannot be effected unless Osiris wants to be healed. That is, unless we can find that spark within ourselves which tells us that 'The Land and its People are One,' and that the world's ills are a direct result of ills within ourselves. Without that insight, no change will occur. The story of Osiris is really one of supreme self-reliance, of will and intent. Osiris, lost within the Underworld, has to realize that he can transform those monsters which threaten him and render him inert and turn them into his purest allies. Wer and Mehen, 'The Most Ancient One' and the 'Encircler' respectively, can be changed from being his serpentine captors into dragons on which he can soar.

The adze, or small plough, which Horus uses to set these outpourings of the New Age in motion, was seen as a symbol of the constellation of Ursa Major, the Great Bear. In the light of the peculiar historical relationship that exists between the peoples of the Eagle and the Bear, American magicians can afford to interpret this on whatever political levels they deem appropriate, given the most recent events.

**I no longer have any idea what 'recent events' this was referring to. Much as I love America I do not go along with the present-day bunch of puerile British politicians and their manufactured idea of a 'special relationship' between the UK and the US. In the 1920s and 30s even**

### ••• the time of the wakening •••

Hitler noted that war between Britain and America was almost inevitable, and he rather hoped to join in on the British side.

To the British mind, however, the Great Bear is King Arthur pure and simple, and much occult work has been done in recent decades with the express intent of Awakening the King, and bringing in the Age under his aegis in some way. What magicians have aimed for as individuals or groups is a Second Coming, no more, and no less. Perhaps not in the focus of a single individual – which would be disastrous at a time when all individuals have to learn to shoulder their own burdens – but via the incarnation of numerous highly-developed souls all attuned to a similar frequency, so to speak, and making their impacts in the realm of science in particular. But science with a heart this time.

I remain extremely optimistic about the world. If my generation is often referred to as the Third Age, then I realise, now, that the term New Age can be used in quite a specific sense: as referring to those young folk we have spawned. All of them much nicer than me and my lot ever were. And their attitudes toward their fellow man are much kinder, less judgemental and far more tolerant. Plus, 50 years ago mystics talked rather archly and cautiously about the 4th dimension; the non-mystics raised their eyebrows in despair. Now, the new generation of scientists talk glibly about the Strings and Superstrings with 10 (or is it 11?) dimensions and no-one bats a third-eyelid.

In Arthurian/Celtic terms, the imagery and inner-plane energies known as Lancelot/Gawaine have cut those furrows into the soil of our consciousness. In these furrows, seed-ideas have been planted. While in the Egyptian system, it is Horus who will rule the new Aeon and restore Maat to the World. This is a case of the Hawk, which brings order back into the world, covered with and soaring by the feathers of

*The Serpent King from Abydos*

Maat, and restoring humanity to a new balance with its environment.

The result, however, is not a foregone conclusion. Before that can happen, there will be yet more turbulence and bloodshed, more confusion and self-seeking. This is because humanity is now experiencing a surge of sexual energy and awareness comparable to what we as individuals know at puberty. This surge will make possible the crossing of the interval between humanity's childhood and the onset of adulthood. But, as Maat would say, the whole thing hangs on a feather. It all depends on whether we can awaken the Horned God within us, so that the Hawk can soar and one day take us to the stars.

These stars, in fact, represent one of the few things that most magicians can agree upon. They argue that our true home is to be found among the stars, and that we do not really belong on this planet at all. Hence the profound feeling that many of us have that we are 'outsiders.' The true 'Fall,' they contend, was caused by 'interbreeding between anthropoid humans and a far superior race from another solar system many millennia ago.

It is a glorious notion, but an uncomfortable one, given the lunatic fringe that such an approach immediately conjures up. However, it is made a bit more acceptable by the suggestion that these 'star people' came to Earth not via spacecraft but as 'viral infections,' space-hardy germs. These could have been carried on meteors, perhaps. Each germ might then have characteristics that worked themselves into the genetic structures of the apelike creatures they infected.

I first heard this idea – or its cousin – over twenty years ago while sitting wide-eyed, young and nervous in the cramped study of a formidable English magician who told me of this while cranking up the pressure on his antiquated paraffin heater. Years later, many years later, the highly regarded and utterly respectable astronomers Sir Fred Hoyle and Chandra Wickramasinghe caused a minor controversy and swayed some pundits when they suggested much the same sort of thing as the most likely origin of human life and consciousness, as well as many epidemic diseases.

Other magicians, however, stick to the more usual notion in which Earth was visited and colonized by several intelligent races from distant star-systems, some of which had distinctly animal-like features – which accounts for the true origins of the Egyptian Gods. A gutsy modern magician, Murry Hope, acting as the medium for her Paschat, or 'Lion People' communicators on the inner planes, says that the links are to be found between Earth and the systems of Andromeda, Auriga, Orion, and Sirius – especially Sirius.

**There is another sense in which we are all are all Star Born. Every atom of oxygen, carbon, iron and the calcium in you was created in the core of a star. These nuclei connect us with the very stars and the history of the stars. We are – all of us – made up of stuff that was forged in the heart of a star. As Carl Sagan said somewhere: 'The cosmos is also within us, we're made of star-stuff. We are a way for the cosmos, to know itself.' So we discover that particles can be in two places at once, everything that can happen does happen, and movement is an illusion.**

**As Aleister Crowley said: 'Every Man and Woman is a Star.'**

However we look at it, and however it happened, it is asserted that the true Sangreal, or Blood Royal, sprang from some sort of contact with these beings. 'This created a genetic strain which carried on the very best of human capabilities allied with good spiritual influences. This strain, it was felt, has considerably influenced our state of civilization for the better, inculcating an unusual element of self-sacrifice among its holders for the sake of spiritual immortality.' And then further: 'It was once regarded as exclusive to certain noble families, but long ago was known to have become extremely widespread, albeit in varying degrees in different individuals.'[50]

---

50 William Gray, *op. cit*

Can we believe this? We can if we want. We can all find these stellar genes within us if we need to. In the simplest terms, the Star-Seed/Sangreal/Blood Royal is energized at that moment when individuals, lost within the morass and terrorized by demons of their own making, decide that enough is enough, that they must rise, that there has to be something beyond or above to which they can relate. That is true initiation, and the beginning of all magic. The Star People can take care of themselves. For the moment, just getting out of the hole is the best that we can begin to do. Once we make this decision from the heart, then all systems and interpretations become unified: The Blood Royal begins to pulse within the veins, the antlers or horns begin to grow, the eyes of Osiris flicker open – and the dawn of a New Aeon begins perpetually anew.

# SIX

# Endings and Beginnings

When I first met the Horned God, I was 24 years old, far younger than my years, newly married and already feeling doomed – a prime example of what was once called a 'callow youth.' My one mark of distinction, as I thought of it myself, was an obsession with magic that had endured for most of my conscious life. But even here, although I had much knowledge, there was little wisdom; ample imagination but no real insight or understanding. I did not even know the Horned God existed, much less what he stood for.

**Looking back I realise now that the goat-like atmosphere of the omnipresent Pan contact I made when losing my virginity, and when having sex out of doors since, was very different in tone to the singular contact my young self is about to describe. Then, I sensed the goat-foot god; this next time I actually saw one of his cousins.**

My first wife and I were a couple doomed from the start: a Chinese pragmatist and a Celtic dreamer do not make the best of bedfellows, even if we did at times love each other with the sort of determination that is really the heavy lid that keeps down despair. I very much knew Atum in those days – we both did. Two dark mounds that occasionally signalled to each other across an emptiness. No faults, no wrongdoing, no recriminations – just different worlds.

In times like that, you tend to find the Horned God. This is not so much through any process of occult research, or magical evocation. It is more akin to the way the Nile recedes, so that you feel as if all the vitality of the dream world has drained away, and there is only thick mud all around, and a cold, thin air where once there had been the currents and shoals within the flow of life itself. He is there, if you know how to look, if you know how to brush off the mud and dirt.

It was in Earls Court arena in the heart of London, where I first saw him: a vast cavern of a building where they have dog and horse shows, boat and home exhibitions, and where the Royal Family come once a year to be dutifully bored to their back teeth by those interminable military extravaganzas which the Old Boys put on for their entertainment.

The Rolling Stones were in concert for that particular occasion, however, and we had tickets, procured with some difficulty. Not because we particularly liked the Stones' music – I had always been a Cat Stevens, Bob Dylan, Paul Simon man myself – but because we were drawn to the myth. Everyone of my generation had to see the Stones at some time. They were seminal. They were definitive. They were 7 pounds a ticket.

Now the Stones were late in appearing, as they always were. The thousands in the audience were restless but good-humoured. The mysteries of ancient Gods were the last things upon my mind just then. That was when the fanfare began. A sound of trumpets echoed and echoed around the hall. I had never heard the piece before and assumed it to be something classical. Then, suddenly, it was all forgotten. Time and place gave way to one of the purest visions of my life. Beneath the huge arch of the ceiling, amid the indefinable but tangible atmosphere of sexuality that was loose within the audience, within the stink of smoke, and dope and alcohol strong enough to support the roof, the Horned God came riding into my vision. Clear and potent and intensely alive, he came riding a dark horse from out of the depths of some primeval forest, into the bright sunlight at its edge. He looked at me across the worlds, across the years, and I was lost to him from then on.

Herne? I thought, or seemed to hear. Although I had little myth then, and less learning, the name was accurate enough, as we have seen. As the music of the fanfare rose and fell and faded away, a door leading to something wonderful opened within my psyche. The Crown of Thorns and all the associated Christian Mysteries ceased to bother me so much. Gradually, surely, it was the God with Horns who began to claim me.

For the rest of the evening in the outerworld, Mick Jagger's prancing on stage around a huge, pink, inflating penis seemed rather silly and completely irrelevant. Moons had arisen within me and nothing was likely to be the same again. Part of me died, but part of me gave birth to something at the same time.

**That sounds pretentious now, but it was true enough. It was in fact an initiation. The symbolism of the forest edge is a potent depiction of that 'place' in your psyche where you can meet up with Otherness. I called that inner contact Herne because that is the name that sprang to mind, but it could also have been named Lailoken, a mounted stag-priest that is wild aspect to Merlin.**

You can invoke him (i.e. give a simple Hello!) every time you go through a certain door, every time you cross an appropriate threshold or find yourself standing on the edge of something. What is that poem by that horny little rascal Guilliame Apollinaire...

Come to the edge, he said.
We are afraid, they said.
Come to the edge, he said.
They came to the edge,
He pushed them and they flew.
Come to the edge, Life said.
They said: We are afraid.
Come to the edge, Life said.
They came. It pushed them...
And they flew.

We need not wait to pushed before we learn to fly.

The real initiations have nothing to do with ceremonies and rites, bells, books and candles. They come in moments of your personal life when you feel propelled toward the edge of something, or else walk toward this edge with the determined sense that holy magic is going to happen.

The music, as I later learned, was Aaron Copland's 'Fanfare for the Common Man' – an entirely appropriate title, as I now realize. And in the light of the Fertility Cult which once rippled outward from the Horned God's image, Jagger's performance on stage was an unconscious piece of mediumship that aptly celebrated a lesser-known God. Herne was alive that night within me. It was the best 7 pounds I ever spent.

He was to crop up again later, over the months and years, but most of the time he was forgotten completely in the need to live a normal life, try hard at my first marriage, and earn a living as any mortal has to. His most vital appearance actually came a few months after the first, bursting into my inner gaze in the lush gardens of the Manor Hotel in Castle Combe in Wiltshire – a village which had once been voted the prettiest in England, and suffered ever since. *Dr. Doolittle* had been filmed there, as I later learned,[51] which, considering the Horned God's role as Lord of Animals, was surely an example of the wry humour that only he can manifest. Really, it was a simple enough encounter: a tall friend of mine stepped under some antlers that were fastened onto a shed wall: but then he seemed to disappear and, for a brief and unforgettable moment, a priest from the oldest light stood before me, filled with the God.

But it was not until 1981 after my wife and I had bowed to the inevitable and separated – mercifully without children to complicate the matter – that the Horned God began to impinge upon my psyche on a regular basis. In fact, the pressure intensified toward the end of that year until I found myself staying awake night after night, filled with a compulsion to draw and re-draw his image in immense size but with tiny detail. I drew these with simple black and white lines without

---

[51] The first dire version, starring Rex Harrison. Harrison himself stayed at the White Hart Inn, nearby, during filming.

shading, without depth – which perhaps mirrored the state in which I then found myself in those lonely days. Such a compulsion to draw invariably marks the awakening of the right hemisphere of the brain, and is a signal that some greater mysteries are on the way.

They were, and I attempted to write them up in an ultimately unsatisfactory book entitled *Gate of Moon*. For long nights in the heart of winter, within the heart of the Western Lands, I lived with the Horned God's image daily – with him and Fiân, which was the name to which his consort seemed to respond.[52]

They never said anything in words. No axioms, no precepts or philosophies. Yet they taught me things somehow, and I would wake from sleep with knowledge that was completely new to me, but which I felt I had known all my life.

Michelle came into my life then, and with her a radiance that was like a smile. She was thirteen years my junior but a thousand years older. I had last seen her in the 17th century when we had had a rugged and impoverished life as farm workers, living near the village of Marshfield in Wiltshire.[53] We buried as many children as we managed to raise. But before that, if we look at it in linear terms, we had shared a considerably brighter world beside the Nile, where I had been a minor scribe and she a young priestess. That night, in January of 1982, she turned up on my doorstep and asked me if I would like to take her for a drink. I would, and did, and our marriage and our many children followed on at decent and entirely respectable intervals.

**Sad sad sad on re-reading those words, done in the early days of love. I did warn her before we went out together that when I was 50 she would look upon me as a wrinkly old man, and want to find someone younger. As it was I was 48 when it happened. Still, sitting here in my Zen garden some 17 years after the split, truly and deeply happy with my third and fey and adored wife Margaret, I can accept that I probably deserved the bad things that have happened to me; the multitude of good things I probably haven't deserved. So this is all a matter of those Balancings I mentioned earlier.**

---

52 Pronounced *fahn*.
53 I still get a curious 'bell-jar' effect whenever I go to Marshfield, as if I'm somehow separated from the rest of the world while being fully engaged with it.

All you young 'uns out there, listen... You can have the Knowledge and Conversation of your Holy Guardian Angel, the visions of the Machineries of the Universe, know the sound of one hand clapping and be able to climb the Enochian Aires from Tex to Lil – and still not have a clue about managing your love life.

In those first years, we rented a tiny old cottage on the middle slopes of a steep valley, where a fold in the earth and a trick of the trees which encircled us gave the area a micro-climate all its own. It was always warm, snow never lasted more than a morning, and the wind through the trees further out made it sound like the ocean lapped to our door. Deer would come down the path; badgers and squirrels would dig out our crops; pheasants would strut upon our wall. Every now and again a great black dog would leap from nowhere into our garden and muzzle around as if it owned the place. While every night, as the Moon soared high above the hills, darkness and silence would encircle our home in a way that showed they were living entities too, deserving our acknowledgements. At two separate places within the large and rambling garden, I came across what I can only call the 'Gates.' Through these, on certain occasions, I was quite certain that I could have stepped right through into the faery realms – quite literally. Without a wife and child, I would have done so.

In fact, I believe that these Gates and opportunities only open fully to those who do have such considerations and concerns. It is all part of the Law of Exchange.

This was the enchanted Murhill, which formed one side of the landmass I think of as Winsley Hill. Extraordinary things happened to me there, and it inspired numerous tomes. All written while holding down demanding full-time jobs in the real world. Something I'm satanically proud of now, although the truth is my books never sold enough copies to make a living from them.

I have to put a large white rock in the very centre of my Zen garden to represent what is my holiest place, although it must seem quite unexceptional to anyone. I rake more than half way around its edges, to represent the way the River Avon caresses it, and muse upon myriad wonders.

It was during this period, when our first child was growing up and I was learning to use the elf-wands given me by Dusty Miller, that I seemed to have plugged into what I can only call the Pagan aspects of a Magical Current that was originally worked within the Stella Matutina, and which was (in many strange ways) linked to energies within the hill on whose slopes we lived. Synchronistic events of staggering scope and complexity, involving awesome levels of coincidence, unfolded with such frequency that I became almost blasé. But at least I learned to take it all as a sign that the Horned God was alive and indeed a-hunting. People accused me in those days, too, of being wonderfully psychic. So I was, and so I am, but I tell many more lies now than I ever used to. This is all part of the roguish, trickster, coyote aspects of Herne. It is really no great problem. The best magician I ever met was not averse to spinning the odd yarn or three.[54]

Then Herne showed me that life on the land is never an idyll, that the least it demands is hard and unremitting graft, with no place for the arrogance of self-pity, or the luxury of despair. He showed me the dark and cold things too, without which the light can have no reality, nor the warmth any power to heal. But those are parts of another story, and not for anyone else. This too is part of the Law of Exchange, the Balancings of Maat.

It was not until the spring of 1989, long after we had left the cottage to live upon another part of the hill, that various strands of magic that had been bothering me for some time all seemed to coalesce at once, triggered by a chance encounter with a delightful lady witch of my acquaintance, who spent a few minutes chatting on a variety of topics while the lock of the nearby canal filled with the murky black-green water. "Did you know," she asked, "that the well and spring near your village is known as the 'Spring of the Green Man'?" I didn't, no I didn't and it was like a blow to the head as a multitude of concepts

---

54 I wish I could remember who I meant! More than one, believe me.

and personal experiences which had apparently no relationship all came together at the same time. I went to the well in question, and the spring which flows from it, tidied up the debris, and sat back to build up the great and 'green' images of Herne and Fiân, sat on a rock and listened like a little boy while they spoke to me of their relatives and ancestors, and saw how they were all within me – within us all.

**Having spent 20 years building the Kabbalistic Tree of Life into my aura, as you were supposed to do if you were to get anywhere in magic, I realised at this period in my life that I needed to spend the next few years rooting it out. I really did aim to become something akin to an Old Earth Man to whom the structures and strictures of the Kabbalibosh, as I came to call it, were irrelevant.**

At this juncture in the original manuscript the American publishers Llewellyn insisted that I add a How-To section. It didn't feel right, but they had always been kind to me so I went along with them. Despite insisting to the readers that the process of Not Knowing and Silence was a superb means of entry into the realms of the Horned Gods, I then preceded to give a series of techniques that were full of Noisy Knowingness.

I have always found that such procedures made sparks for me on a one-off basis only, like matches. Likewise, similar techniques offered by other writers on magic rarely worked for me at all.

So all that remains to do now is open a few doors, unlatch a few gates. The Horned God and his Lady do not ask a great deal from us in the way of actual techniques. They are not overly fond of dogma. On the whole, unless you catch them in the Osirian mode, they would rather not have the elaborate ceremonial that many magicians insist upon creating.

In fact, they really only need two small things from us: a knowledge that they exist and a determination to make contact. Although perhaps we can add a third – the quality of respect. Not worship, not blind adoration, just simple and dignified respect is quite enough for any man, woman, or deity.

Everyone's approach toward the Horned God must necessarily be different. The important thing is not what you do, or how cleverly you do it, but the fact that you are doing it at all. This is Osiris rousing himself, deciding that he must quit the night and come toward the day. This is Herne coming to the edge of the primeval forest, under a similar compulsion. It is Arthur – and any other sleeping hero – rousing himself because he knows that a time has come.

When it comes to raising the Horned God, the crucial factor depends on the efforts made by the seekers themselves – not via the specific techniques and formulae of an established cultus, but through their own ingenuity. It does not matter how crude and indeed silly the first attempts at making an inner contact are. It is the courage to make the attempt in the first place which the Horned God seeks. He will respond in kind. Do no more than slavishly copy the methods of established practitioners and all you will get is a kind of dull, Otherworld golem. Use your own creativity and you will touch upon the Horned God in the full flow of his power.

Each person reading this now contains within him or herself all that is needed to make a genuine, transformative contact with our oldest deity. Knowledge and determination are the actual dynamics which will get us started via some exceedingly simple first steps:

Research the Horned God and his Lady in public libraries, draw their images – no matter how crudely – from whim and fancy.

Look out for the stag/hart/deer/ram/horned animal motifs in the outer world.

Make a note of everything.

That is the start, nothing more. If you have the guts, the balls and the 'fire within,' you will realize in later years that every step you make toward the Horned God, the Horned God is making toward you.

But you have to want this to happen with all your heart.

With all of your hart.

---

**It is said that after death you have a period in a kind of astral limbo in which you see replayed everything that ever happened in your life. You then make a detached, non-judgmental assessment of what lessons you might need to learn in the next incarnation.**

I dread this. Working in my Zen garden has been hard enough at times when my rake has brought up lost memories and past follies. I dread to see the many moments when I have acted with all those faults for which that singular being known as Man has been lambasted: crass stupidity, unwarranted arrogance, incidents of low-grade self-justifying cruelty, unnecessary small-minded nastiness and moments of unforgiveable cowardice on many levels. Yet it is all there before me, within the low walls, amid the shadows of the rocks and the gravels, making me wonder what I might need to learn for whatever is left of this life.

What advice can I give my new readers, young magicians, when it comes to making Zen gardens of their own?

Switch off, as I am doing now. Breath. Look around without internal comment. Breath again. See beyond the walls...

What do I see?

I see the edge of a vast forest of oak, ash and thorn, the tree tops swaying like waves, and surging up behind them a range of high, clustered hills, some with beacon fires of secret peoples and their hidden lives. And beyond them, even, the jagged snowy tips of huge mountains enfolded by the swaying, electric-blue and faery-green dancing goddesses of the Aurora Borealis.

The spaces between the trees before me are crowded. Apart from the sullen Templars (who look disturbingly like present-day Taliban) there are horned beings of every sex; slithering dragons with folded wings; a single old centaur; men and women with the heads of jackals, lions, hawks and ibises; actual deer, stags, foxes, crows and a black dog; a pregnant, tattooed Bronze Age priestess called Lleuadd, with Pytheas the Mariner; a very sexy Boudicca with her two daughters; witches, wizards and cunning men from every century; a few lonely and rather lost Celtic Christians; Dion Fortune walking hand-in-hand with Maiya, her Sea Priestess; Christine Hartley and Colonel Seymour, the latter bursting with unexpressed sexual tension; nameless, unknowable, ever-young and shimmering members of the Sidhe; the infinitely fanciable Moina Mathers, who to my crass schoolboy senses is the Top Toff Totty of the Western Mystery Tradition...

It is heaving with wonders in there. It glitters. Contains every possibility. What I have learned from re-reading *Earth God Rising* is that the whole premise of the Divine King and the Old Religion is probably more right than wrong. And even if it was/is all 'vapid balderdash', yet it is eminently workable, full of life, light and love – and exploding with irresistible charm.

I look down at my austere, sterile Zen garden and see it now as something rather sad, almost pitiful. There are weeds coming up between the stones. Shall I rake them away? What was it Dion Fortune said? "A weed is just a misplaced flower." These new flowers grow before my astonished gaze. Looking closely I see ice blue petals with golden stars in their centres: forget-me-nots. As I start to remember, it becomes clear that in a few short moments fertility will have taken over from sterility.

I stand up and straighten, suddenly feeling young again. There is something happening at my feet but I dare not look. I suspect they are becoming cloven; they are certainly sinking deeper into the ground. Meanwhile the walls of my little Zen garden, having been built without foundations, tumble over and are consumed, becoming one with the earth. Breathing deeply, feeling stronger than I have felt in many years, I snap the head off my rake and turn the shaft into a very useful walking staff, or a cudgel, or yet a wand for working bold magic.

Some of the beings in my primordial forest are beckoning. Others, in that timeless realm, are just waiting patiently. There are sounds of music – are they pipes? – and much laughter. There is entrancement in there: a siren song, a faery song, which even I who am hearing-impaired can dance to because the notes are pounding in my blood rather than my ear-drums.

I step through the remains of my Zen garden; it is little more than a slight rise in the ground now, lush with wildflowers jostling for the sun.

In the Eleusinian Mysteries and within the Hermetic Order of the Golden Dawn they would begin a ritual with the words: 'Hekas, Hekas, este Bebeloi', which meant 'Far, far from this place be the profane.' Here, now, and in your heads, I would suggest calling out to all those unseen beings, energies and potentials who are waiting for us to make contact, the simple Words of Power:

"I'm coming in! Don't start without me!!"

www.ingramcontent.com/pod-product-compliance
Lightning Source LLC
Chambersburg PA
CBHW020803160426
43192CB00006B/426